ICE

The Earth series traces the historical significance and cultural history of natural phenomena. Written by experts who are passionate about their subject, titles in the series bring together science, art, literature, mythology, religion and popular culture, exploring and explaining the planet we inhabit in new and exciting ways.

Series editor: Daniel Allen

In the same series

Air Peter Adey

Cave Ralph Crane and Lisa Fletcher

Clouds Richard Hamblyn

Comets P. Andrew Karam

Desert Roslynn D. Haynes

Earthquake Andrew Robinson

Fire Stephen J. Pyne

Flood John Withington

Gold Rebecca Zorach
  and Michael W. Phillips Jr

Ice Klaus Dodds

Islands Stephen A. Royle

Lightning Derek M. Elsom

Meteorite Maria Golia

Moon Edgar Williams

Mountain Veronica della Dora

Rainbows Daniel MacCannell

Silver Lindsay Shen

South Pole Elizabeth Leane

Storm John Withington

Swamp Anthony Wilson

Tsunami Richard Hamblyn

Volcano James Hamilton

Water Veronica Strang

Waterfall Brian J. Hudson

Ice

Klaus Dodds

REAKTION BOOKS

To my parents

Published by Reaktion Books Ltd
Unit 32, Waterside
44–48 Wharf Road
London N1 7UX, UK
www.reaktionbooks.co.uk

First published 2018

Printed and bound in China

A catalogue record for this book is available from the British Library

ISBN 978 1 78023 905 7

CONTENTS

Prologue

For those of us living in more temperate and tropical environments, ice comes in and out of our lives. Here today and gone tomorrow. Ephemeral in nature. Go back in time, however, and the experiences of ice are quite different. In 1814, Londoners enjoyed for the last time an impromptu 'Frost Fair', a legacy of the five hundred years of cooler weather labelled Europe's 'Little Ice Age'. *The Times* reported on 2 February 1814, 'in some parts the ice was several feet thick, while in others it was dangerous to venture upon.'[1] Enterprising watermen led the revellers back and forth across frozen water, as they enjoyed games, feasting and drinking. It was not the first such fair, as others had occurred in the seventeenth century. The frigid winter of 1962–3 ushered in the refreezing of the Thames and the accumulation of sea ice off the eastern British coastline. But it did not match the frolics of 1814.

While ice can and does melt and disappear, it leaves an indelible mark on things it comes into contact with. So making sense of ice and snow means being attentive to multiple temporalities and spaces. The North American continent was bequeathed with a set of 'Great Lakes' because of it and they remain in place regardless of whether those waters are frozen or not. The iconic Yosemite Valley is probably one of the most prominent glaciated landscapes. Its legendary El Capitan rock has an elevation of some 2,300 m (7,500 ft). This spectacular feature owes its existence entirely to past glaciation. The ice made its mark on weaker rock but was forced to work its way around

Unknown artist, *Frost Fair on the Thames, with Old London Bridge in the Distance*, c. 1685, oil on canvas.

7

the comparatively ice-resistant granite core. Much admired by tourists, its distinctive and rugged topography created an inviting challenge to generations of climbers and later BASE jumpers.

The United Kingdom's landscapes, including its highest mountains Ben Nevis and Snowdon and glaciated valleys in the Lake District National Park, owe their existence to ice and snow falling, taking up residence, moving and melting. As Nan Shepherd notes in her literary masterpiece, *The Living Mountain: A Celebration of the Cairngorm Mountains of Scotland*, we are surrounded by 'the elementals' – the elemental power of ice, snow and water coming into contact with rock and sediment.[2] Dame Barbara Hepworth, the great twentieth-century English sculptor, spoke of 'landscape sculpture' and 'the feel of the earth'. This seems fitting when contemplating the legacies of ice and snow.[3] U-shaped valleys, fjords, mountain ridges and striated surfaces on rock surfaces all offer testimony to that erosive power. Ice abrades, plucks, carries and deposits rock, water, soil, fauna and flora elsewhere.

El Capitan, Yosemite National Park, California, United States.

Our relationship with ice

We have an ambivalent relationship with ice and snow. The mathematician Johannes Kepler marvelled at the snowflake's perfect six-cornered symmetry and in the early seventeenth century contributed to modern understandings of the structure of crystals.[4] The nineteenth-century American poet Henry Wadsworth Longfellow wrote of the beauty of the falling snowflake and contributed to a Romantic sensibility, which took pleasure in the intrinsic beauty of ice:

> Out of the bosom of the Air,
> Out of the cloud-folds of her garments shaken,
> Over the woodlands brown and bare,
> Over the harvest-fields forsaken,
> Silent, and soft, and slow
> Descends the snow.[5]

Glaciated valley in Borrowdale, Lake District National Park, Cumbria.

While the tiny snowflake inspired scientists and poets alike, speculation about ice sheets, ice caps and sea ice fired geographical imaginations. Were there, as Aristotle believed, 'frigid zones' which book-ended the temperate and torrid climatic zones?[6] We have a rich legacy of maps and charts that offer insights into how our ancestors envisaged those 'frigid zones'. And we have a litany of written and visual accounts of first-hand encounters with nature's ice. As a young medical doctor, later novelist of crime, Arthur Conan Doyle wrote about his experiences of the Arctic while on board a whaler. But he also penned a fictional account entitled 'The Captain of the

The physical hexagonal structure of snowflakes.

Subterranean map
of the Antarctic
continent showing
East and West
Antarctica.

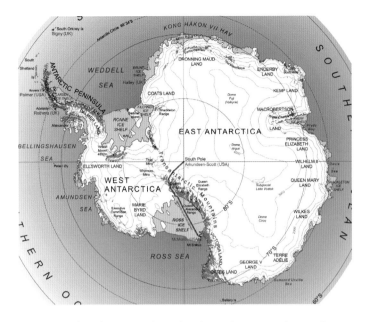

Pole-Star' (1833), which describes how the captain's vessel goes
mad and eventually walks to his death over the sea ice. In Conan
Doyle's literary imagination, ice is where white European men
simply go mad.

Nowadays, scientific advances involving ice cores and satellite mapping mean that we can engage with ice in very different
ways. Modern ice maps are far removed from their ancient Greek
and European Renaissance counterparts, tracing as they do
underlying geological structure and surface contours. They add
height and depth and bring a distinctly volumetric appreciation
of ice and snow. It is perfectly possible to spend an entire career
looking at and listening to ice without ever having to experience
it directly.

For all our enhanced understanding of ice, a cornucopia of
awe, pleasure, loathing, fear and revulsion endures. Children
might enjoy snowball fights and skating while parents fume
about disruption to their journeys to work. But there was a time
when it was only the very privileged among us who enjoyed add-
ing fruit and sugar to fresh lumps of glacial ice harvested from
Norway and the European Alps. Consuming ice was considered

*overleaf: Theatrum
orbis terrarum* (Theatre
of the World) printed
in May 1570 with the
Arctic and Antarctic
imagined as vast,
frigid, ice-covered
zones.

TYPVS ORE[

Estotilant.

ANIAN regnum.

CIRCVLVS ARCTICVS.

AMERICA SIVÆ IN-
DIA NOVA. Ao 1492. a Christophoro.

Tolm   Colombo nomine regis Castellæ primum detecta.

Noua
Franc.

Chilaga   Cia.

Tuchano
QVIVIRA regnu.
Quivir

Cenis   Totonteac   Ceuola

And   Teuhtear   Cruola

Tontonteac

Canones insula   C. del engaño

Calicuas   Tagil

Florida.

La Bermuda

La Emperadada

Marata

Las dos hermanas   L las Bolcanes

Malabrigo   La surfana

TROPICVS CANCRI

Archipelago di
Zamai.   Restinga di
ladrones   Rocca
partida   S.Thomas
Anubiada

Abreojo.

Las iardines
S.Lazaro.   Inf. de los corales.

Inf. de los reyes

J. de hombres blan   CIRCVLVS AEQVINOCTIALIS   J. de los galapegos.

Caribana.

La barbada
Las Bolcanes   Iris di los Tiburones.

Tisnada

Nova Guinea
nuper inuenta
quæ an sit insula
an pars continentis
incerta est   MAR DEL ZVR   Insulæ
incognitæ

Pe ru.   Amazones.   Brasil.

ins. di S.
Pedro.

TROPICVS CAPRICORNI.

EL MAR
PACIFICO

Chili   Chica   Rio de la Plata

Hanc continentem
Australem, nonnulli
Magellanicam regionem
ab eius inuentore nuncupant.

Chile.

Archipe
lago.

CIRCVLVS ANTARCTICVS.

Terra del Fuego.

190 200 210 220 230 240 250 260 270 280 290 300 310 320 330

TERRA AVSTR

a marker of sophistication rather than something commonplace or even mundane. Ice has been a healer for centuries, treating swelling, sores and wounds.

We still find examples aplenty of our ambivalent relationship with ice throughout the world. In Swedish, if someone reports that they are feeling 'under the ice' (*under isen*) then the listener would reasonably presume that they were feeling 'under the weather', as their British counterparts would say. In Spanish, the phrase *quedarse de hielo* implies a sense of astonishment, with ice (*hielo*) being used to invoke the involuntary reaction of the body to shock – akin to someone putting an ice cube down your back without warning. In Korean, residents refer to a 'normal winter' as *sam-han-sa-on* (three cold, four warm), meaning that after three cold days it is not uncommon to enjoy four warmer days if the cold Arctic currents from Russia change prevailing direction. In Chinese, being 'ice- or snow-smart' is considered a compliment.

In English, we put ice to work in a variety of ways, using it to describe aspects of human character and behaviour and revealing the intersections with gender, race, sexuality and nationalism.[7] For women accused of being 'assertive' or 'unemotional', epitaphs such as 'snow queen', 'ice dragon', 'frigid' and 'ice heart' are put to use. Ice is thus associated with an undesirable personality type, such as that which the British American pop group Foreigner sang about in the 1977 song 'Cold as Ice'. But 'snow queen' is also used as an anti-gay slur to refer to black gay men who prefer white partners. We might, as the film *Top Gun* (1986) reminds us, refer to an 'ice man' (a white straight man) and imply a positive persona that remains 'ice cool', regardless of the pressure. But how often do we hear women being described as 'ice cool' rather than 'frigid'? And when we speak of 'pure as the driven snow' we have William Shakespeare's Hamlet to thank for another gendered ice-bound epithet occurring in Act III, Scene I: 'Be thou as chaste as ice, as pure as snow, thou shalt not escape calumny. Get thee to a nunnery, go.'

We chide children and even adults for 'skating on thin ice': inferring that their actions and behaviour are close to the boundaries of social acceptability. Arguments and actions that fail to convince us 'cut no ice', and if we underestimate a problem we are told that we have only grasped the 'tip of the iceberg'. We talk of 'ice-breaking' with its origins in the sixteenth century referring to safe passage through river ice. Nowadays we use it to refer to activities designed to bring people together, especially those who have not yet met one another at conferences and workshops. If a Swedish speaker says 'there is no cow on the ice' then they mean to reassure us that there is nothing to worry about.

The idiomatic flexibility of ice is in keeping with the material itself. Icebergs are solid objects that float on their liquid version and are created when pieces calve off from large bodies of ice and float in oceans and lakes. The popular adage 'tip of the iceberg' is germane because 90 per cent of an iceberg is submerged. Generally speaking, icebergs refer to pieces of ice more than 5 m (16 ft) in width. On the one hand, they represent a hazard to shipping and are capable of sinking ships. On the other hand, iceberg tourism is popular in places like Newfoundland and Labrador where it is common to see hundreds of icebergs offshore as a consequence of calving from Greenlandic glaciers.

The durability of an iceberg will depend on the interaction of atmospheric and subsurface air and water temperatures alongside wind action and surrounding sea ice. Warmer waters will cause subsurface melting, and warmer air temperatures can encourage snow melt and the development of melt ponds. Surface melt can then encourage further cracking and the eventual demise of the iceberg. But we should not underestimate their size either. At their biggest, icebergs are breathtaking. An iceberg that carved off Antarctica's Ross Ice Shelf in 1987 was estimated to be around 6,300 square km (2,432 square mi.) in area and up to 1.4 trillion tonnes in weight. The latest worry concerns the possibility of a new 5,000-square-km (1,930-square-mi.) iceberg forming in the aftermath of an enormous crack being discovered in the Antarctic's Larsen Ice Shelf.

Even when you might not be looking for it, ice can be found everywhere, even in equatorial mountain environments such as the Rwenzori Mountains in the Congo and Uganda.[8] We

have also found ways to make, move and store ice, which has complicated our love–loathe affair with it. In the 1930s and 1940s, fridges and freezers were beginning to make their presence felt in homes, hotels and restaurants. In 1949–50, the owners of Mohawk Mountain Ski Resort in Connecticut were the first to excavate 700 tons of ice and 'top up' their ski slopes in the midst of a mild winter. The creation of artificial snow then followed. The snow cannon was unveiled in 1952 and first used at an upstate New York ski resort. Subsequently, it has been re-branded a Snowmaker. While it consumes a great deal of energy and water, it helped to keep many a ski resort viable while elsewhere global warming is blamed for melting naturally formed ice.

Rwenzori Mountains, Uganda.

Down to Earth

Without comets composed of water ice, we would not have had the oceans that we now take for granted as being integral to the history of the Earth. Water ice is not, therefore, something unique to Earth. Comets from outer space brought the world's oceans to Earth. Further afield, astrophysics has revealed that other planets in our solar system owe their origins to the intersection of gas and dust, rich in the very stuff that makes water possible, namely oxygen and hydrogen. Some planets such as Mercury and Venus are relatively bereft of water thanks to their proximity to the Sun but the impact of comets was a game-changer for Earth.

The Snowmaker (full blast cannon at the Nordic Centre, Canmore, Alberta, Canada).

Our closest planet, Mars, also has polar deposits and a climate history that bears similarities to Earth's. At the poles of Mars, scientists have identified ice caps and evidence of permafrost elsewhere. The surface of the planet is punctuated

by landforms that are believed to have been created by past glacial action, indicative of climatic shifts. Mars's polar latitudes,
and what is termed polar layered deposits, have invited further
investigation after high-resolution photographs were secured
from NASA's Mars Reconnaissance Orbiter. The images revealed
icy worlds similar in size to Greenland rather than Antarctica.
The water ice deposits are buried beneath layers of dust, snow
and gaseous ice. In winter, temperatures are estimated to be far
colder than Antarctica at over minus 120°C (minus 184°F).

Further afield, and thus more remote from the Sun, water
ice was and is more prevalent both at the surface level and the
subterranean. The largest planets, Jupiter and Saturn, have identifiable ice moons. Most recently, high-resolution pictures of
Pluto, released in July 2015, revealed a mountainous dwarf planet
with ice peaks as high as the North American Rockies. Jupiter
has an ice moon called Europa, which possesses a layer of ice
over a frozen surface believed to be masking an active ocean.[9]
Remarkably, the surface temperature of Europa is estimated to
hover around minus 160°C (minus 256°F), some 80–100 degrees
colder than the interior of Antarctica in the winter season.
Within the rings of particular celestial bodies such as Saturn, ice
dust and even substantial boulders of ice are known to circulate.
Without the near continuous bombardment by meteorite material, those rings might have remained lighter in colour and
thus more distinctively icy to the human eye. Saturn's moons
contain ice as well, and NASA's space vehicle Cassini detected
water vapour escaping from the surface of one of those moons.
Ice deposits are also detectable on Mars, Mercury and the
Moon, and icy comets float through our entire solar system.

The presence of ice anywhere in the solar system sparks
rumination about the possibility of extraterrestrial life, providing material for futurists to imagine human colonies extending
on to other planets within our solar system. But ice can also
come from outer space and make its presence felt on Earth. In
1908, a fragment of comet-ice fell from space and landed with
an enormous bang in Siberia, itself no stranger to ice and snow.
What made this impact remarkable was the sheer scale of it

– a lump of ice so substantial that scientists estimate it to have been equivalent to something that had not been invented yet – an atomic bomb explosion. Over 2,000 square km (772 square mi.) of forest were devastated and it is not hard to imagine what the impact might have been had it fallen, say, on a city such as Moscow further to the west.

Ice and our earthly geographical imagination

In this book, the reader is taken into the imaginative and material worlds of ice and snow. Entwined with cartographic, literary and scientific realms of ice are further human worlds of images, memories, heritage, folklore and literary musings. Our literary worlds have been greatly enriched by poems, stories and ruminations about ice and snow. Many British children grow up with Raymond Briggs's story *The Snowman* (1978) and perhaps later encounter the poetry of William Wordsworth and Ted Hughes in the tale of 'Lucy Gray' (1800) and 'Snow' (1956) respectively. The wonder of snow falling on the window is caught beautifully in James Joyce's *The Dead* (1914). For Joyce the snow is a malleable and precarious link between the past and the present and between the living and the dead. As the final paragraph notes,

> It was falling, to, upon every part of the lonely churchyard on the hill where Michael Furey lay buried. His soul swooned slowly as he heard the snow falling faintly through the universe and faintly falling, like the descent of their last end, upon all the living and the dead.[10]

Holocaust survivor Primo Levi wrote in the 'Last Christmas of the War' (1986) about how the snow, ice and bitter cold of the concentration camp in December 1944 affected him. At first Levi writes of the inconvenience posed by the icy cold to his work as a laboratory technician in the camp:

> It was snowing, it was very cold, and working in that laboratory was not easy. At times the heating system

didn't work and at night, ice would form, bursting the phials of reagents and the big bottle of distilled water.

But later he speaks of how a blockage caused by ice precipitated a series of events that led to an unlikely encounter with a German laboratory technician and an impromptu bicycle repair.

A few days later, toward the middle of December, the basin of one of the suction hoods was blocked and the chief told me to unplug it. It seemed natural to him that the dirty job should fall to me and not to the lab technician, a girl named Frau Mayer, and actually it seemed natural to me too. I was the only one who could stretch out serenely on the floor without fear of getting dirty; my striped suit was already completely filthy . . . Since my hands were already dirty, she asked, could I fix her bicycle, which had a flat? She would, of course, give me something for my trouble.[11]

The intrusion of ice led to a small 'reward' from Frau Mayer of sugar and eggs to the starved Levi.

For film buffs, murder mysteries such as *Murder on the Orient Express* (1974) and horror movies such as *The Shining* (1980) owe their dramatic power in large part to the protagonists being

NASA Galileo Orbiter shows two views of the trailing hemisphere of Jupiter's ice-covered satellite, Europa, 7 September 1996. Left: approx. natural colour appearance; right: false colour composite version.

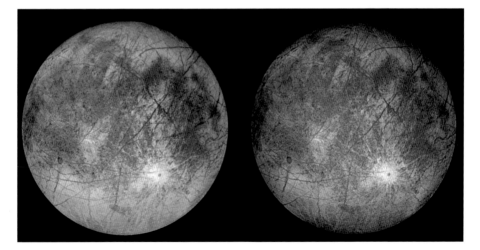

Piz Gloria, Schilthorn, Switzerland (as featured in the 1969 film *On Her Majesty's Secret Service*).

trapped and isolated by ice and cold. John Carpenter's *The Thing* (1982) warned us that the capacity of ice to store and preserve alien life carries with it unwelcome consequences. The release of alien life in Antarctica leads to the overwhelming of an American party trapped on a scientific station. Even for the last survivor, death appears a welcome prospect in the wake of a burning base, multiple deaths and little to no prospect of rescue. Television shows and films such as *Dr Who* ('The Ark in Space', 1975), the Austin Powers series (1997–2002), *2001: A Space Odyssey* (1968), *Sleeper* (1973), *Coma* (1978), *Alien* (1979) and even a *South Park* episode assembled storylines involving cryonic hibernation and storage. Spy thrillers such as *On Her Majesty's Secret Service* (1969) and *The Bourne Supremacy* (2004) use ice and snow to either showcase the skill set of hero figures or to convey the splendid isolation of the evil genius's lair. For the polar explorer, the shamanist and the fantasy novelist alike, ice and snow are literary and oral alchemy – turning ordinary stories into epics. Hans Christian Andersen's *The Snow Queen* (1844) suggests, 'It was a lady; her cloak and cap were of snow. She was tall and of slender figure, and of dazzling whiteness. It was the Snow Queen.'[12] Nepalese, Tibetan and Indian shamanism feed off a rich oral tradition of mysterious and mountainous creatures: the Yeti, the undisputed lords of the mountains and forests. Assuming various shapes and sizes, the most widely represented is the Nyalmo, a high-altitude-living and large carnivorous beast capable of killing Yak.[13]

We make demands on ice, too. While we use it to conjure up mystery and excitement, we also want to be able to use it and live with it. The indigenous hunter on Arctic sea ice wants to travel safely on it. Sports fans want to watch their teams glide and slide over it. Architects, engineers and planners are expected to design and manage it. Militaries want to be able to dominate it. We also want to be able to preserve it and the things that it supports in the name of heritage. People living in the highest city in the world, La Rinconada in Peru, work in a gold-mining economy surrounded by ice. While comparatively few people live and work with ice on a near-permanent basis, many millions of people and wildlife depend upon melting ice and snow for their drinking and agricultural water. Some may never see it or feel it, but without it their lives would be so very different.

In some ice-bound places, we even hope for higher standards of behaviour on and under it. Antarctica is governed by a special, even unique, arrangement and is often touted as a model of resource management, where humans have to share with one another. The Arctic region is one of the most peaceful areas in the world, with the eight Arctic states (Canada, Denmark/Greenland, Finland, Iceland, Norway, Russia, Sweden and the United States) working co-operatively with one another on areas of mutual concern such as conservation and search and rescue.

It is a two-way street, however. Working together in ice-filled areas is laudable but if we hasten ice's demise, then there will be consequences for all of us, human and non-human alike. Darker surfaces absorb more solar energy. Melting ice sheets contribute to global sea-level rise. Low-lying coastal flood plain communities and cities become vulnerable. Diminishing sea ice in the Arctic Ocean might open up new trading routes and resource opportunities, but that might be little comfort when compared to the global consequences that will follow. A world with less ice and snow will produce its own winners and losers, in a context where ten billion people will be calling Earth their home by the end of this century.

Before it all goes, at least in its natural form, we will glide and slide over its diverse physical geographies (Chapter One), the human exploration of ice and snow (Chapter Two), the imaginative and aesthetic qualities of ice (Chapter Three), ice and geopolitics (Chapter Four), working with and on ice (Chapter Five), leisure and pleasure on ice (Chapter Six) and finally, adapting to ice (Chapter Seven). It is not exhaustive but it should offer a *tour d'horizon* of a remarkable substance, which allows us to bridge and connect human and non-human histories and geographies over millennia. We can articulate and exercise our hopes and fears for the future not only on our home but elsewhere in the solar system. Ice is integral to the human condition.

1   A World of Ice

What is ice?

Ice is frozen water. Glacial ice is quite different to more regular ice, including artificially made ice cubes. The compacted crystalline structure of glacial ice means that it absorbs every other colour (such as red and yellow light) in the spectrum apart from blue or turquoise. So the net effect is that it appears quite different to normal translucent ice, which reflects all visible light back without apparent preference. Blue light is the only form of light able to penetrate below its icy surface. What also makes glacial ice quite unlike ice cubes harvested from the freezer is that it will contain impurities such as rock, soil, plant and bacterial matter. It will be more than just simply frozen water.

But there is much more to it than that. Ice can take multiple crystalline forms, and it can resist the usual freezing point of $0°c$ ($32°f$) at lower pressures. It can carve and shape things like rock and soil, it can reflect back solar energy, it can float on water, and it plays a crucial role in the determining the Earth's energy balance.[1] Ice never forgets its origins. It is a substance after all which is perfectly capable of turning back into water. If ice endures then it can shape-change. As a mover and shaker, it can excavate, spread and deposit. It can and does support life below and above its surface as fish, seals, polar bears, whales and smaller life such as algal meadows and microbes attest. Subglacial lakes buried under Antarctic glaciers and ice sheets are the latest extreme environment to attract scientific attention because of the possibility to investigate which microorganisms might endure.

Snow is formed when the atmospheric temperature is at or below freezing and moisture in the air begins to freeze. On reaching the ground snow may persist depending on the ground temperature and surface conditions. Ground-level snow struggles to persist if surface temperatures go beyond 5°c (41°f). Without moisture, however, it is perfectly possible for very cold and dry environments such as the Dry Valleys in Antarctica never to experience snowfalls.

The presence and distribution of ice and snow are shaped not only by prevailing environmental conditions such as moisture, wind and temperature but also by the crystal-like structure of ice. Using low temperature scanning electron microscopes, scientists better understand how ice forms once it absorbs atmospheric moisture. Under laboratory conditions, researchers have reproduced ice crystal formation via time-lapse photography and extraordinary microscopic capacities. Sample particles of around two microns in size, far smaller than the width of a human hair, are carefully nurtured in specialist research chambers. The end result is research that is leading to improved understanding about how ice crystals form in the atmosphere and develop a crystal-like structure.

Ice is most commonly crystallized in a symmetrical hexagonal structure. The water molecules are arranged in hexagonal rings. The hexagonal structure reflects molecular behaviour,

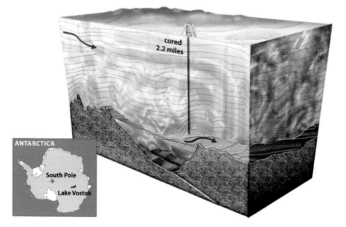

Artist's impression of subglacial lakes under Lake Vostok, Antarctica.

which favours a pattern based on maximizing attractive forces.   Ice crystals.
Symmetry brings with it the prospect of greater molecular stability. While the water molecules in ice and snow form hydrogen
bonds with one another, and form this distinctive hexagonal
structure, there is always variation within snowflakes and ice.

Atmospheric conditions such as temperature and humidity ensure that no snowflake is entirely identical. As pressure increases on ice, the standard hexagonal structure of ice crumbles and the hydrogen–oxygen bonds alter to form denser crystal structures and thus allow for even greater diversity of ice structures.

The novelist Anthony Doerr wrote in *About Grace* about an obsessive Alaskan-based hydrologist, David Winkler, who fixates over the beauty of ice crystals. His prose captures well the dedication required in ice crystal research. As the narrator explains:

> as a graduate student, he eventually found the basic design (equilateral, equiangular hexagon) so icily repeated, so unerringly conforming, that he couldn't help but shudder: Beneath the splendor – the filigreed blossoms, the microscopic stars – was a ghastly inevitability; crystals could not escape their embedded blueprints any more than humans could. Everything hewed to a rigidity of pattern, the certainty of death.[2]

Maybe the American novelist had in mind the laborious work of the twentieth-century Japanese glaciologist Ukichiro Nakaya or the earlier work of the American photographer Wilson Bentley. Nakaya's beautiful book *Snow Crystals* (1954) first showed the intricate pattern of ice crystals that he had discovered and then artificially created in his laboratory at Hokkaido University in snow-covered northern Japan from 1936 onwards.[3] He spent hours taking thousands of photomicrographs of natural snow crystals collected around Sapporo and then patiently identifying different types via photographic plates. Nakya was inspired by Bentley and his posthumous publication, also titled *Snow Crystals* (1931). Both men offered public audiences insights into the beauty and complexity of the snow crystal. Bentley and Nakaya took thousands of photographs of snow locally sourced in the United States and Japan respectively. Bentley used a bellows camera on top of a microscope. Scratching off the black emulsion from the negative, he was able to retain the shape of the snowflake.

Tragically in Bentley's case, ice and snow accounted for him as he died of overexposure to a freezing blizzard while walking home.

Locating ice

Physical scientists refer to the ice-covered environments of the Earth as the *cryosphere*, a portmanteau word from ancient Greek: *kryos* (cold, ice) and *sphaira* (sphere, globe). The cryosphere is that part of the Earth's surface that is seasonally or perennially frozen, and as such it shapes and structures the physical environments of the Arctic, Antarctic and mountainous regions in particular.[4] Our knowledge about ice, and where it has been found in the past and present, comes from a range of sources including ship- and land-based observations, whaling ship logbooks, newspaper reports, aerial surveys, and more latterly satellite observations and ice cores.

Ice and snow can be found anywhere, as freak weather and strange temperatures have been known to overturn received wisdom about where and when ice should be encountered. In December 2013 winter storms in Jerusalem amassed some 38–50 cm (15–20 in.) of snow, which would be enough to cover the lower slopes of an Alpine ski resort. Perversely, snow and ice may not be present when we might expect it to be. In April 2015 Californian authorities reported for the first time that there was no snow to be recorded in their annual survey of snow and ice at Echo Summit in the Sierra Nevada Mountains.[5] About a third of the state's water reserves are dependent on the annual snowmelt from that mountain range alone.

Ice is not restricted to the Arctic, the Antarctic and the world's mountain ranges, as shown in Table 1. Around 10 per cent of the world's surface is always covered in ice. But beyond glaciers and ice sheets, we have lake and river ice, sea ice, ice caves, permanently frozen ground (also known as permafrost) and icebergs, as well as ice crystals in the atmosphere. Ice can be trapped underwater in lakes and oceans and as stalactite-like structures attached to the underside of sea ice and icebergs. Snow nourishes

Aerial view of the Greenland ice sheet.

glaciers and ice sheets by transmogrifying from *firn* (frozen snow lying at the surface of glaciers which is partially consolidated by alternate freezing and thawing) to ice.

The key forces complicit with the making and remaking of ice are wind, water, brine and other minerals, terrain and temperature. Ice is found almost everywhere, and might even be found inside the Earth itself. The global cryosphere (the frozen water part of the Earth's system) is geographically dispersed. Over 50 per cent of the world's glaciers are in the Arctic region but the largest in the world is in Antarctica, namely the Lambert-Fisher glacier, which is over 400 km (250 mi.) in length and close to 100 km (60 mi.) wide.[6]

The world's biggest ice bodies are Greenland and Antarctica. They represent 95 per cent of the world's total volume of land ice. The Greenland ice sheet encompasses 1.7 million square km

Components of the Cryosphere	Area covered (million square km)	Ice Volume (million cubic km)	Potential Sea Level Rise (cm)
Snow on land (Northern Hemisphere) (annual min–max)	1.9–45.2	0.0005–0.005	0.01–1
Sea ice, Arctic and Antarctic (annual min–max)	19–27	0.019–0.025	0
Ice shelves	1.5	0.7	0
Ice sheets (total)	14	27.6	6390
Greenland	1.7	2.9	730
Antarctica	12.3	24.7	5660
Glaciers and ice caps (lowest and [highest] estimates)	0.51 [0.54]	0.05 [0.13]	15 [37]
Permafrost (Northern Hemisphere)	22.8	4.5	-7
River and lake ice	(n/a)	(n/a)	(n/a)

(close to 700,00 square mi.), which is roughly 80 per cent of the area of the island and is equivalent in size to the African country of Sudan. The Antarctic ice sheet is breathtakingly large, extending to some 14 million square km (5.4 million square mi.) and containing around 24.7 million cubic km (6 million cubic mi.) of ice, which in places extends to over 5 km (3 mi.) in depth; it is substantially larger than the second biggest country in the world, Canada. It is common to distinguish the Antarctic Peninsula, East and West Antarctic Ice Sheets because of their distinct characteristics. The bedrock underneath the West Antarctic Ice Sheet is significantly below sea level and it is believed to be unstable compared to its eastern counterpart because of contact with warmer oceanic waters.[7]

Table 1: global cryosphere.

Global figures for ice needed varies from season to season. Snow and ice cover varies, and its loss in the spring and summer seasons is the biggest variable factor in its global distribution. The only permanent snow cover is limited to the interior of Greenland, the polar ice caps and the highest mountains; but permanent does not imply unchanging. The overall mass of snow and ice will depend on the relationship between accumulation and ablation. The Greenland ice sheet experiences loss through ice discharge and surface melt. There is hemispheric variability, however, with the southern hemisphere (excluding Antarctica) enjoying far less snow and ice coverage than its northern counterpart. The South American Andes, Southeast Australia, New Zealand and a few East African mountains are the main sources of snow and ice in the more southern latitudes, and critical in terms of providing water resources for humans, flora and fauna.

Antarctica does experience surface melting but it is the area of the world where we can be most confident in asserting the presence of perennial ice; even then glaciers and ice shelves will experience losses through bottom melting and calving as they come into contact with warmer ocean waters.

The weight of ice sheets is so great that if they were removed we would be looking at parts of a world physically depressed by hundreds of metres. What we know from past research on earlier eras of postglacial rebound is that the effects are not immediate when ice is removed in huge quantities from surrounding landscapes. So it is not as if the Earth would move dramatically or immediately. What is termed isostatic adjustment conveys what might be at stake: namely, a period of short-term and longer-term adjustment and change. Earthly movement would be both upwards and downwards as changes in sea levels, the gravity field of the Earth and even some crustal movement take effect. The physical geographies of the Earth would change as sea levels rose and as ice continued to disappear. Twenty thousand years ago, sea level was about 130 m (430 ft) lower than it is today, largely due to an ice sheet that covered most of North America.

Ice sheets contain old and new ice, with the oldest from the Pleistocene, a vast geological epoch stretching back some 2.5 million years and ending around 10,000 years ago when the Earth entered an interglacial period. The height of the Greenland and Antarctic ice sheets rivals mountain ranges around the world. The highest point in Greenland lies at 3,200 m (10,500 ft) and in central Antarctica, it is not uncommon to be about 4,000 m (13,000 ft) above sea level. The ice extends downwards, depending on underlying geology, to over 3,300 m (11,000 ft) and 4,780 m (15,600 ft) in Greenland and Antarctica respectively. Over 80 per cent of Greenland is covered in permanent ice, which explains why human settlement remains on the coastal fringes of the island. In the case of Antarctica, the figure is even higher and permanent ice covers over 99 per cent of the total surface area. The Transantarctic Mountains effectively slice through the polar continent, separating a thicker and higher body of ice in the east from one that is low-lying and warmer due to its proximity to the South American mainland and warmer air and water currents. The one significant exception is the Dry Valleys area in East Antarctica, which, due to its unique microclimate, resembles a lunar and predominantly ice-free environment.

Glaciers and ice sheets are the most significant sources of ice. As a consequence of weight and gravity, the eventual fate of ice will depend on the relationship between accumulation/collection and ablation/melting. As snow lands on ice sheets and glaciers it is buried, compressed and transformed into glacial ice. Glaciologists think that there are over 200,000 mountain glaciers, ice fields and ice caps around the world.[8] In the European Alps alone, 54,000 glaciers have been identified.

Ice sheets, glaciers and ice caps can and do melt. Surface melting is becoming more common in the summer season on the

The McMurdo Dry Valleys, Antarctica.

inland Greenland ice sheet and the Antarctic ice sheet in Western Antarctica. Satellite imagery and airborne photography are vital accomplices in the monitoring and assessment of glacial bodies, as is the mapping of ice thickness through airborne and surface radar surveys. Repeat photography historically played a crucial role in recording glacial retreat and advance, and in identifying separate glaciers and ice fields. Most have been discovered at high latitude but the Patagonian ice field, as a mid-latitude ice field covering 16,000 square km (6,200 square miles), demonstrates that latitude alone is not a reliable indicator of where huge ice fields can be found. But estimating glacial stability and volume is not straightforward and requires careful consideration of a plethora of factors, including glacial surface melting, ice loss due to calving, and dramatic events such as avalanches.

The reported melting of the large Patagonian ice field proved catalytic to further scientific investigation. Using satellite observation data stretching from the 1970s to 2000s, scientists found that the ice field was losing volume and thinning at even the highest elevations. As melting has accelerated, it is estimated that the Patagonian ice field is contributing now around 0.07 mm (0.003 in.) per year to global sea-level rise, which represents a shift from a figure of around 0.04 mm per year in the 1970s and '80s.[9] Warming air temperatures are thought to be indicative of change because if rain falls on glaciers, as opposed to snow, then there is more opportunity not only to melt but to alter the overall balance of glacial systems, ultimately leading water to infiltrate and undermine glacial stability. But as we shall see, ice is under assault and rain is not the only culprit.

Types of ice

While ice sheets, glaciers, ice shelves and ice caps are most significant in terms of global size and scope, there is a bewildering diversity of ice. It can take many forms depending on location, ambient temperature and disturbance. It is common to distinguish between airborne, land and marine ice; and then we can identify further types of ice such as fast ice (sea ice attached to the shoreline), pancake ice (separate pieces of sea and lake ice), brash ice (the hardest bits of glacial ice) and frazil ice (soft ice that fails to harden because of its location in cold turbulent water).

We have developed an enormous vocabulary to describe ice and its properties rooted in both Western science and traditional indigenous knowledge. In the Inuit language of Inuktitut, there are about a dozen (rather than hundreds as some might presume) basic words pertaining to ice including *siku* (ice), *aniu* (snow used to make water), *aputi* (snow on the ground) and *qinu* (slushy ice close to the sea). Those basic words can be supplemented by a portfolio of words pertaining to sea ice such as *qautsaulittuq*, which is ice that breaks after being poked with a harpoon, and *iniruvik*, which is ice that cracked because of tidal changes and then refroze. As Inuit in northern Canada and Greenland are dependent on hunting and fishing on and close to the edge of the sea ice, a successful hunter needs to be an ice detective, capable of assessing and predicting the density, viscosity, spatial extent and thickness, age and solidity of ice. Inuit consider themselves to be part of a constant and lively exchange with ice, water, snow and wind.

Both Western scientists and indigenous hunters have marvelled at the beauty and diversity of ice. Ice crystals, which are created when the warmer air above the ground intermingles with lower colder air, are a good example. When these bodies of air come into contact with one another, the water vapour in the warmer air causes an increase in humidity and if sufficient it can cause ice crystals to form. Described as diamond dust, and similar to a light foggy day, it is very thin and rarely affects visibility in a way that freezing fog can and does. As a consequence of its delicate composition, the tiny crystals appear to glitter and it seems like diamonds in the sky are falling to earth. Greenlandic Inuit call ice crystals *patuktuq*; they attach themselves to the faces and clothing of hunters travelling across the sea ice.

While beautiful to watch, ice crystals are a comparatively minor element in ice typology. In polar, alpine and marine environments, permafrost, or permanently frozen ground, is the most significant in terms of its impact on human communities. To qualify as permafrost the temperature of the ground must be below 0°c (32°F) for at least two years. Vast areas of the inhabited world, including northern North America and northern and western Russia, areas of Mongolia and western China are affected by permafrost. Eighty-five per cent of Alaska has permafrost, as do around 50–55 per cent of Russia and Canada.

Diamond dust ice, Antarctica.

Less visible than sea ice and glacial ice, permafrost varies from 1–2 m (3–6 ft) thick to around 200–300 m (650–980 ft) thick in many parts of the affected world, depending on underlying geology, soil, snow cover, organic content, salinity, local pressure points that determine melting, levels of human disturbance and surface temperature. The thickest permafrost in the world was recorded in northern Siberia around the Lena River, extending to around 1,500 m (5,000 ft) and containing some of the oldest ice in the world. Marine permafrost is found on the cold continental shelves of the Arctic basin, while alpine permafrost is found in places like western China and in the Andes in the southern hemisphere. Permafrost stability depends on the active layer, a zone close to the surface that is subject to freeze–thaw cycles.

River and lake ice are more familiar to residents and communities outside the Arctic, Alpine and Antarctic worlds. It is not uncommon for rivers such as the Charles in the city of Boston in Massachusetts to be frozen over during the winter months. Where river ice is thick enough, recreational activities such as ice skating and even ice fairs have flourished. Depending on temperature, water mixing and currents, river and lake ice can persist for weeks. Surface melting can also create congelation or black ice, where water is refrozen and forms a thin transparent veneer, posing a hazard for those who traverse its surface. Ice-road truckers in Canada and Alaska readily appreciate such hazards when driving over seasonal river and lake ice roads.

Sea ice is the dominant ice type in marine environments. Composed of brine, ice crystals, air and solid salts, its condition is affected by salinity levels, relative melt and the state of ocean currents. Sea ice is highly dynamic and variable depending also on the temperature of ocean water, which is affected by atmospheric and subsurface heat flux. Scientists distinguish between first-year ice that forms in the autumn season and multi-year ice that has endured at least one summer season of potential melting and dispersal. Multi-year ice is thicker as a consequence and far more hazardous to shipping but safer for indigenous peoples to step on to when hunting. First-year and multi-year ice is to be found off the coastlines of the Arctic and the Antarctic. Due to the physical geography of the Arctic, multi-year sea ice is more prevalent because ice is trapped in the Arctic basin, whereas Antarctic sea ice tends to drift northwards into the warmer waters of the Atlantic, Indian and Pacific oceans where it disperses. In the Arctic, there is a dominant direction of ice flow and accumulation due to the circulatory movement of water in the Arctic Ocean and sea ice can literally be jam-packed in areas around the Canadian and Greenlandic Arctic while being relatively clear off the coastlines of Russia and Norway.

The distribution and condition of sea ice is uneven; some areas can experience melt ponds where there is surface melting due to the reflective cover of the ice being altered, possibly by pollutants. But it is also common to find areas of open water called polynyas in between sea ice, where wind, pressure and ocean conditions have literally 'opened up' gaps in coverage. Sea ice rheology remains a work in progress as scientists continue to probe how it shears, deforms, ridges, fractures and disappears. Sea ice investigation requires satellite coverage and the use of automated underwater vehicles (AUVs) in order to evaluate spatial extent and ice depth respectively. Analysis of water chemistry and temperature will provide further clues as to why and how sea ice experiences variability in thickness and extent.

Albedo and energy balance

The intersection between atmosphere, the cryosphere and the substrate determines whether snow and ice settle and endure or simply melt and disappear. The 'life expectancy' of ice is integral to planetary albedo and the Earth's energy balance. Albedo refers to the amount of sunlight or radiation reflected by a surface. Snow is the brightest natural surface on the planet and has an albedo approaching 0.9, meaning around 90 per cent of solar energy making contact with snow is reflected back into the Earth's atmosphere. But deciphering trends and trajectories of albedo change is not straightforward. For one thing ice continues to surprise us. A simple example comes from the glaciers connected

Sea ice with visible melt
ponds on the surface.

to Mount Everest which are covered with surface debris such as rock, dirt and dust. Not only is the local albedo of the mountain being affected, the surface paraphernalia is acting as an unwelcome heat reservoir, encouraging surface melting and ice loss.

Ice, if covered by a layer of snow, is judged to have the highest albedo level of close to 1, meaning a perfect reflector of solar energy. What the layer of snow does is further delay summer season melt and keep ocean temperatures lower. By way of contrast, a score closer to 0 would imply a darker surface where a very high level of solar energy was absorbed. Water, in contrast to ice, absorbs heat and is thus less reflective. So the relationship between ice and water in the world's oceans, especially the Arctic and Southern Oceans, is critical because it plays a crucial role in determining both regional and global ocean temperatures. Sea ice has a high albedo (0.5–0.8) compared to open water (as low as 0.05); in sea ice up to 80 per cent of its solar energy is reflected away from the surface. If ocean waters continue to warm, then any remaining sea ice is inevitably in jeopardy.[10]

Ice intermingles with the solid, liquid and vapour states of water. Each interacts with the Earth's atmosphere and environment in their unique ways. Snow is found in the atmosphere where ice crystals form and as they begin to develop and gain mass eventually drift towards the ground because of gravity. What will determine their eventual fate is the prevailing temperature in the troposphere, the lowest band of the Earth's atmosphere. Within this zone, the fate of our weather is decided because 99 per cent of the atmosphere's water vapour resides there and depending on what is unfolding in that part of the sky we will be showered with snow, hailstone, rime (derived from freezing fog), freezing rain, frost and/or sleet.

It is something of a lottery but whatever happens the fate of those snow crystals begins to be sealed by a triumvirate of temperature, humidity and wind. For those that fall to the ground, their shape and form are capable of considerable mutation. Ice crystals are works of beauty and their initial hexagonal-prism-like appearance can and does morph into column-, needle-,

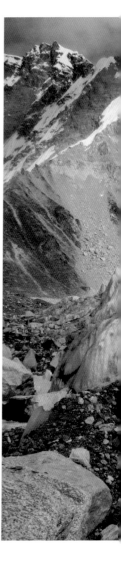

Glacial debris is now a major area of academic research, including in the work undertaken by the NASA Goddard Space Flight Center at Khumbu Glacier in the Nepali Himalayas.

plate- and dendritic-like structures. Ralph Waldo Emerson recalled 'the frolic architecture of the snow' and 'north wind's masonry' in his poem 'The Snow-storm', highlighting how snow and ice could reveal evidence of their distinct morphology.[11]

Understanding ice and 'ice ages'

Over the last four hundred years, our understanding of ice has been transformed by exploration, discovery, observation, analysis and modelling. The German cartographer and geographer Sebastian Munster's *Cosmographia* (1544) and the Swiss theologian Josias Simler's *De Alpibus commentaries* (1574) were the earliest to reflect on the lively and dynamic nature of ice and ice bodies such as glaciers. Later researchers used the Swiss Alps as their intellectual testing ground. Johann Scheuchzer (1672–1733) posited that glaciers were mobile rather than static bodies of ice; the explorer and mountaineer Horace-Bénédict de Saussure (1740–1799) was convinced that glaciers could advance and retreat depending on climatic variations. The Scottish geologist James Hutton (1726–1797) observed that glacial shifts in the European Alps were responsible for dumping and depositing rocks and boulders over large areas. These early glaciologists were highlighting a physical world on the move, and one that was not simply carved and sculpted by biblical forces.[12] In his *Theory of Earth* (1788), Hutton introduced to readers the idea of 'deep time' and the principle that the Earth was the sum of long-standing and ongoing forces, including erosion, uplift and deposition.

The Swiss geologist Louis Agassiz (1807–1873) became the undisputed champion of 'glacial theory', a catch-all term to describe the view of glaciers as movers and shakers of alpine environments. His work, entitled *Etudes sur les glaciers* (1840), kick-started systematic scientific reflection on glacial dynamics and behaviour.[13] The British scientists James Forbes and John Tyndall became prominent in advocating theorizations of past ice ages and ice viscosity. In the twentieth century, new associations such as the Association for the Study of Snow and Ice (1937) were established in the UK with the aim to involve both scientists and citizens in ice and snow survey research. In one scheme, observers living in upland areas of Britain were asked to record snow levels on postcards and send them to the association's headquarters in Edinburgh.

The Swiss glaciologist
Louis Agassiz
(1807–1873).

Late nineteenth-century and twentieth-century advances in radiometric dating offered exciting opportunities to advance Hutton's insights regarding 'deep time'. In 1913 Arthur Holmes in his *The Age of the Earth* posited the idea that dating rocks via radioactive decay could help date the genesis of the Earth. Holmes thought initially it might be 1.5 billion years old. Three decades later, scientists were suggesting that the earth was 4.5 billion years old. Disciplines such as geology, glaciology and climatology used radiometric dating to begin to reconstruct past climates and by the 1940s were able to establish that there have been five so-called ice ages in the Earth's history (Table 2).

What we call an ice age is a shorthand term for a lengthy period of time (often millions of years) where global temperatures have been cold and where large areas of the Earth are populated with glaciers and ice sheets. During the ice age, global temperatures and ice distribution and thickness vary and thus it is possible for ice to advance and retreat. Our most recent ice age was the Quaternary, which began about 3 million years ago (and ended some 11,000 years ago). The earliest has been dated to around 2 billion years ago using climate reconstruction methods including ice coring, rock analysis, landscape evolution and environmental proxies such as fossils and pollen samples. Modern techniques such as isotope analysis (which focuses on different types of oxygen found within objects) reveal that global temperatures have varied by as much as 5°C (41°F) and in some cases by more than 20°C (68°F).

For the last 11,000 years the Earth has enjoyed a relatively stable climate with ice largely concentrated in identifiable ice sheets and glaciers. Global warming is making its presence felt, and earth scientists study ocean and atmospheric circulation patterns because past research suggests that shifts have been responsible for ice ages in the past. Plate tectonics can also be significant because anything that interferes with the flow of warmer water from the equator to the polar latitudes will in turn shape ice formation. Unsurprisingly, warming seas and oceans interfere with sea ice extent and thickness. We know this from many decades of research on past climate reconstruction using

Table 2: Five ice ages.

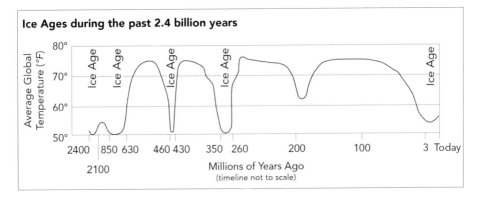

ice cores (in some cases with ice that has been extracted several kilometres into ice sheets) and studies of landscape evolution. Current monitoring of ocean and air temperatures, flows and patterns is crucial to future detective work.

One thing we have learned, above all else, is this – ice ages can and do end suddenly. They might take a while to make their presence felt on Earth but climate history suggests that abrupt and sudden change is not unusual. *The Day After Tomorrow* (2004) may have revealed all the exaggerated tendencies of the disaster movie genre but it did point to something important. Time is significant. An ice age can end in a few short years and when it does global temperatures can alter dramatically, maybe by much as 10°c (50°f). By the end of the movie, dramatic change in the Earth's climate had left New York under ice rather than flooded by rising sea levels.

Ice under siege

The fate of ice is a worry for all of us regardless of whether we encounter it or not. The Intergovernmental Panel on Climate Change (ipcc) reports continue to chart notable and persistent trends including that atmospheric concentrations of carbon dioxide, methane and nitrous oxide are now higher than in the last 800,000 years. In essence snow and ice act as a thermal radiator control, moderating and modulating atmospheric and oceanic warming. Polar amplification and accelerated warming at higher latitudes disrupt the palliative care that planetary ice can offer. Snow and ice are on the frontline of climate change and while seasonal snow cover is expected to vary from year to year, there is now growing evidence that it is simply being lost year on year.

Glacial decline has profound implications for water resources, regional and global climate, and accompanying alpine and polar ecologies. Precipitation is not the only threat to ice, as studies of sea ice show there are other forces at play including ocean chemistry and heat transfer cycles. Hardly a month passes without some story or other charting the vulnerabilities of ice, with dramatic news that giant ice shelves have collapsed in

Antarctica (such as the Larsen A in 1995 and Larsen B in 2002). In Antarctica, stories tend to congregate around ice shelf collapse, while in the high north attention revolves around shrinkage and melting.

Arctic sea ice was thicker and rougher in previous decades, and melt ponds on the surface of sea ice are worrisome. Melt ponds matter because they absorb far more of the Sun's heat per unit area (because of the presence of water bodies) than ice. Sea ice cover, especially multi-year ice, blocks the transfer of ocean heat to air during the autumn and winter and helps protect Arctic coastlines from winter storms. Sea ice loss means that more ocean heat is transferred to the atmosphere, and an ice-free Arctic Ocean ends up warming with implications for ocean chemistry and biology. The salinity budgets of polar seas alter and the prevailing living environment for fish and other marine life is affected.

The phenomenon of the colour of ice turning from white or grey to black, brown, pink and red is a sign of potential glacial distress. When snow masses are covered in darker materials, including dust and algae, it alters albedo. On the Nepal–Tibet borderlands, scientists have discovered that glaciers such as Ngozumpa were affected by traces of soil, soot and black carbon being deposited on ice and snow. A loss of albedo results in a longer melt season as more solar heat is absorbed. In Greenland, the ice sheet has darkened in the last decade and the melt season extended by up to ten days in recent years. 'Dark Snow' has resulted from forest fires occurring in Siberia and North America. Future climate modelling is destined to factor in ever-greater scope for bio-albedo effects.

When ice disappears it leaves behind a trail of implications and ramifications for all living beings and their relationship to planet Earth. Sometimes subtle, sometimes not so, ice and snow are crucial to so many aspects of life, including weather formation, water release and circulation, salinity budgets, and ultimately species migration and survival. Snow and ice have helped to make our 'hot planet' habitable, a world where ice sheets retreated 12,000–14,000 years ago, leaving Greenland and Antarctica as the only survivors.

Coring ice and climate archives

Over the last 150 years, glaciologists and physical geographers have excavated the ice and snow from glaciers and ice sheets in order to better understand snow accumulation patterns. Nineteenth-century glaciologists, such as the Swiss-born Louis Agassiz, recognized that glaciers held extraordinary insights into the Earth's past because of their sensitivity to temperature fluctuation and that landscapes and glaciated regions offered up important insights into geological and climatological change. For the post-Agassiz pioneers in glaciology, they were literally digging with pick axes and shovels. Later researchers developed ice cores extending some 100 m (330 ft) below the surface in Antarctica as part of the 1949–52 Norwegian-British-Swedish Expedition.[14]

Thanks to the pioneering work of European and American scientists in the 1960s, glaciologists have been able to better appreciate the composition of glacial ice and the information that might be extracted about our ancient world.[15] Ice cores, from Antarctica and Greenland, permit earth scientists to reconstruct past climates extending over hundreds of thousands of years. The extractive process, involving drilling technology developed by the oil industry, helps to secure year-by-year data because as snow and ice accumulates each year it stratifies into a sequence of layers. In the midst of the last glacial cycle, a huge ice sheet covered the northern hemisphere and Antarctica was larger than today. Ice cores reveal the sensitivities that exist between ice, ocean, surface and water temperatures and the implications for living beings, including human communities far smaller thousands of years ago.

Scientists studying the trapped air bubbles in the ice cores gain insights into prevailing atmospheric composition, wind conditions, vegetation, soot and chemical pollutants, volcanic detritus and variations in temperature. We now know that relative proportions of greenhouse gases reveal evidence of past global temperatures, meaning that higher levels of methane and carbon dioxide are connected to higher temperatures. The

Replica of an Otzi shoe.

air bubbles found in ice cores provide clear evidence that the eighteenth- and nineteenth-century industrial revolution and the onset of carbon economies contributed to unprecedented levels of greenhouse gases and resulting implications for land and sea ice. This coincided with the end of the Little Ice Age (between 1300 and 1850).[16]

Deep-time ice cores are extracted from ice sheet regions called domes, containing high-altitude and very cold ice. The depth of the drilling varies depending on the location but it can penetrate downwards for thousands of metres. After extraction, the ice is bagged and tagged and then stored in a freezer until flown to laboratories elsewhere. The ice is then sliced down the middle and the exposed sample prepared for analysis. It is vital that no cross-contamination occurs with any other part of the sample. The water collected from melting is then subject to further chemical analysis, which may reveal traces of elements such as salt and sulphur, indicative of past climatic conditions.

Research continues to involve multinational consortia in Greenland and Antarctica. In Antarctica the 'holy grail' remains the hunt for the 1-million-year-old ice core. Thus far, scientists have been able to reconstruct past climates to around 800,000 years ago. Work undertaken by the European Consortium for Ice Coring in Antarctica (EPICA) secured that particular milestone in the last decade.[17] While the search for the 1-million-year-old ice core may sound gimmick-like, the rationale is grounded in the periodicity of the Earth's climate history. We know that every 100,000 years or so the Earth enters into an ice age, but around 1 million years ago the duration between ice ages is thought to have been considerably shorter, closer to 40,000 years. Why did the interval period shift by some 60,000 years? Was there something profoundly different about the Earth's motion, including its tilt and/or orbit, because any change in tilt and motion carries with it implications for the capacity of solar light to affect the rate and extent of glaciation? A 1-million-year-old ice core might help deliver some definitive answers, and help us understand the intersection of ice ages and inter-glacial epochs.[18]

Future ice

Ice is the keeper of the Earth's secrets. It can conceal and obscure but when it melts it reveals horrific and wondrous insights into our ancestors and their lives. In 1991 retreating glacial ice in the European Alps offered up the frozen remains of a fully clothed 5,000-year-old man called 'Otzi'.[19] Retreating and melting ice in Siberia and North America continues to reveal a cornucopia of animals that made human survival possible, including the majestic mammoth.

The future holds plenty of challenges for glaciologists to grapple with. For all the extraordinary achievements in probing and penetrating beneath our world of ice, there remains uncertainty about how we account for and explain a substance that is also relentlessly dynamic. Every year, every season and every day, the extent of snow, the distribution of ice over water, the prevalence of permafrost and the ice mass budgets of glaciers and ice fields are subject to change. Making sense of natural variability and long-term human-induced impact requires extensive data collection and monitoring over the world's ice-covered zones. It is expensive and time consuming.

We have made extraordinary leaps in our understanding of our 'white planet' and how and where humans and other life forms experienced life with ice. Some did not make it. Others thrived. In the last 10,000 years or so humans have been one of the biggest beneficiaries of a relatively stable climate. A world with less ice means a world where our relationship with Earth is less assured.

2 Exploring and Conquering Ice

Exploration is not the same as discovery.[1] Sometimes discoveries were made by indigenous peoples while visitors such as sailors, adventurers, whalers, sealers and scientists were also notable in this regard. Discovery is an outcome. Exploration reflects a thirst for knowledge, adventure and the promise of wealth. New technologies and devices such as aerial and underwater drones are offering exciting opportunities to explore under and over ice sheets and glaciers. Some of the most exciting scientific research deals with the intersection between water, rock and the subterranean environments of glaciers and ice sheets. Subglacial lakes buried under the ice masses of Antarctica and Greenland suggest that there might even be microbial life in the most unlikely of places.

The discovery and exploration of ice comes in many forms.[2] Human contact with ice led to further discoveries of yet more ice and stimulated theorization on how we might understand its formation, qualities and consequences. Travelling through the polar regions and high-altitude mountains has led to encounters with an array of ice such as frazil (soft ice) and anchor (ice created at the mouth of fast-flowing rivers when they come into contact with very cold seawater), with different shapes, origins and properties; some (but not all) of which are safe and secure to travel over and to camp on. Ice climbing and mountain exploration required an ability to 'read' the ice and ascertain whether it is wise to climb the icefalls, frozen waterfalls and cliffs, and rock faces covered with ice. By the nineteenth century, ice climbers

Sir Edmund Hillary, conqueror of Everest.

began to distinguish between alpine ice (frozen snow) found in mountains and water ice, which is frozen flows of water.

Professional societies such as the Alpine Club, created in 1857 in London, contributed to an experiential archive of ice and snow. Amateur and learned societies such as the Royal Geographical Society (created in 1833) codified and regularized access to specialist knowledge on climbing techniques and equipment. Items such as crampons and ice axes became de rigueur for the modern mountaineer, especially when ice climbing. Techniques such as belaying, leading, abseiling and lowering made it ever more possible to execute successful ascents and descents. By the 1930s, twenty mountaineering organizations would gather in

Chamonix to inaugurate an Alpine Congress. What was to follow was an International Climbing and Mountain Federation (ICMF, established 1947), which commissioned reports on mountaineering, including how to climb over high-altitude ice and snow. Mountaineering in the words of one former president might also play its part in the post-war 'moral reconstruction of the world' by encouraging international camaraderie among climbers.[3] The ICMF developed a widely accepted global grading system in 1968. The hardest climbs are classified as Grade VII+ with ice climbing acquiring its own gradation, with some variation depending on which part of the world one is climbing in.

The conquest of ice and cold is overwhelmingly narrated as a story of white European and North American men striving and struggling to master cold places. Ice and snow act as lively and dynamic spaces, which test the human body and mind to the utmost limits. For those who survived, a world of fame and fortune could await, as a medley of polar explorers and mountaineers became household names. Those who perished, such as Captain Robert Scott and his Terra Nova party, became national heroes solemnly commemorated and celebrated in the UK, Australia and New Zealand. The conquest of Everest in May 1953 by the New Zealand beekeeper Edmund Hillary and the Nepalese Sherpa mountaineer Tenzing Norgay became a moment for Commonwealth and even global celebration, coinciding with the coronation of Queen Elizabeth II.

This chapter starts with the earliest musings about ice, often linked to ideas about the further north and 'frozen sea'. For many medieval Europeans, experiences of snow and ice were part of everyday life in the winter months. Adults and children liked to skate and sledge. So the discovery and exploration of snow and ice in northern extremes, and later in the far south, was made distinct by size and permanence. One of the most notable accounts of northern Europeans was by a Swedish writer and part-time bishop, Olaus Magnus, in 1555, and he reflected on how ice and snow had helped contribute to the hardiness of Scandinavian peoples. In Magnus's account, there are also some of the earliest sketches of ice crystals. From the sixteenth century onwards, European exploration of the Arctic and Antarctic introduced audiences to accounts, images and, later, photographs and film of immense mountains, ice sheets and sea ice. Sailors, mountaineers, commercial agents and polar explorers were instrumental in this exposure of the poles and mountains. The lure of the poles and the scaling of great heights attracted learned societies, commercial enterprises and news media. Eventually, women were also able to access these remote ice-filled worlds and make their 'voices' and experiences felt and heard.

Ultimate Thule?

The Greek adventurer Pytheas of Massalia (now the port city of Marseille in France) is believed to have made an exploratory voyage of northern Europe around 325 BC. Based on a now-lost narrative, *On the Ocean*, it is believed that he encountered the British Isles and discovered what is now spelt 'Thule', the most northern point of the known world, where he might have met sea ice and experienced extremes of light and darkness. Speculation continues to surround his most northerly position but it was probably somewhere off northern Norway, after his journey north of modern-day Scotland and across the North Sea.[4]

Ancient Greek geographers such as Strabo in his account *Geography*, written circa 30 BC, appear to credit Pytheas with identifying for lower-latitude audiences the existence of a frozen sea (*mare concretum*). As Strabo notes, Pytheas spoke of a northerly environment where drifting sea ice was prevalent and that it was 'a six days' sail north of Britain, and is near the frozen sea'.[5] Strabo's description of sea ice was elemental and evocative, 'no longer either land properly so-called, or sea, or air, but a kind of substance concreted from all these elements, resembling a sea-lung . . . which you can neither walk nor sail upon'.[6] 'Sea-lung' refers to the expansion and contraction of a jellyfish as it moves through water. What Strabo was probably describing is pancake ice, a formation of ice that is composed of rounded pieces that mingle and jostle with one another as ocean and wind currents exert their grip on their surface and volume.

Statue of the Greek
geographer and
cartographer Strabo
(64 BC–AD 24).

The mystery over the location of Thule was not clarified by
Strabo's account. Northern Norway, southern Greenland and/or
Iceland were all likely contenders. Like the lost world of Atlantis,
Thule fired the geographical imagination of those who followed
ancient Greek mythology. For some Greeks, the inhabitants of
Thule were northerners living at a gateway to the wondrous
realm called Hyperborea, literally the place 'beyond the northern

winds'. Its inhabitants were spared the curses of ageing and blessed with ample natural resources, including water. It was a benign place filled with forests and fertile fields. Ice, snow and mountains ringed its southern fringes and the god of the north wind, Boreas, was the guardian of this magical kingdom. He could unleash his cold, wintery, ice-filled winds on those who displeased him.

For those brave or foolish enough to enter Hyperborea, there awaited a chilly and dangerous welcome. You would have to cross Pterophoros, a land characterized by permanent snow, ice and an environment we would now describe as tundra. If you survived that, you then faced possible attack by eagle-lions and a fierce tribe of people called Arimaspoi. Beyond those immediate life-threatening challenges, the horrendous-sounding Rhipaion Mountains awaited.[7]

The ancient Roman natural philosopher Pliny the Elder published his *Natural History* in AD 77 and reflected on earlier Greek claims about Thule. In Book 4, in his description of the British Isles, he notes:

Boreas, the Greek god of the north wind and winter.

the most remote of all that we find mentioned is Thule, in which, as we have previously stated, there is no night at the summer solstice, when the sun is passing through the sign of Cancer, while on the other hand at the winter solstice there is no day. Some writers are of opinion that this state of things lasts for six whole months together ... At one day's sail from Thule is the frozen ocean, which by some is called the Cronian Sea.[8]

He repeats the earlier claim that Thule is located six days' sail north of the British Isles, but it is still not entirely clear where the search area might be.

The legacy of Thule was to leave later Europeans with a rich repository of myth, speculation and empirical observation about Europe's northerly territories, including its icy seas and oceans. Thule's exact location remained stubbornly mysterious but whatever it was and wherever it lay, Greek and Roman writers to varying degrees were convinced it did lie on the edge of the known map, that it was unusual in terms of its cycles of light and darkness, and that it might possess inviting treasures. What is remarkable is that for hundreds of years the same basic knowledge recorded about the frozen ocean to the north was being regurgitated in texts, including those penned by the English monk Bede the Venerable in the eighth century. If we were to ask, 'What did the Vikings ever do for us?' then one answer would surely be radically enhancing European understanding of the northern latitudes. While swift to attack and pillage, they were colonizing Iceland, the Faroe Islands and Greenland. By the eleventh century, the Vikings reached the eastern edges of North America. Iceland would appear to be a plausible candidate for Thule, an island that was described by Viking explorers as a land where the ice was found in great abundance covering mountain-tops, floating off the coastline, and darkened and discoloured in the interior because of volcanic activity.

In the Middle Ages and later Renaissance Europe, the quest for 'Ultimate Thule' became a more general rallying cry for European explorers and their monarchical sponsors in Continental

Europe. The fourteenth-century Italian writer Petrarch warned that it might not be worth discovering, let alone exploring.[9] But that did not stop the speculation and intrigue about snow-covered islands and an ice-filled ocean. Informed by the writings of the ancient Greeks and Romans, there was plenty of interest in the world's frigid zones both to the north and south of the European world. In the absence of direct observation and reflection, these frigid zones were imagined and represented as lands and seas with mountain ranges, rivers and other geomorphic features.

The invention of the microscope in 1600 encouraged further exploration of snow crystals, and writers such as René Descartes and Robert Hooke studied and sketched their observations. Armchair scientists could interrogate the internal structure of ice while geographers and explorers committed themselves to finding the ice-covered areas of the earth.

The lure of the poles

Even before the North Pole was allegedly reached in the first decade of the twentieth century, the lure of the Arctic and Earth's northernmost points was embedded in the nineteenth-century public cultures of both Britain and the United States. Eighteenth- and nineteenth-century polar exploration was underwritten by a series of quests including the traversing of the Northwest Passage, reaching the North Pole, hunting for Franklin's lost party, and the crossing of the Greenland ice sheet. As indigenous peoples in the Arctic recognized, and Western explorers and scientists learnt through their own experiences, failure to learn what to look for, to hear and to feel could be a matter of life and death; the difference between falling into frigid water, slipping into an unforgiving crevasse, or sliding down a vertiginous mountain slope. As stranded men starved, as in the case the Franklin and Greely Expeditions in 1845–6 and 1881 respectively, it became clear that cannibalism could not be ruled out.[10]

The Norwegian explorer Fridtjof Nansen deliberately allowed his ship, the *Fram*, to get stuck in the Arctic sea ice between 1893

The 1881–4 Greely Expedition (also known as the Lady Franklin Bay Expedition) and the ship *Proteus* dropping off supplies to the expedition members at Lady Franklin Bay, Nunavut, Canada.

and 1896 in the hope that he and his expedition might slowly drift towards the North Pole. Informed by oceanographic studies into ocean and wind currents, he understood the Arctic Ocean to be a slow-moving platform of ice and, with sufficient patience, a conveyor to the terra incognita of the North Pole. It was slow going, however, and insufficiently captivating to audiences who wanted to hear of 'dashers' rather than 'drifters'. What drove Nansen's curiosity was the belief that the high Arctic might even be ice free, if warmer currents were sufficient to ensure that sea ice could not congregate. Nansen's drifting voyage proved decisively that there was no 'open sea' in the high latitudes.

Nansen's discovery in the late nineteenth century brought to a close earlier dreams about Arctic seas being passable. The Russian explorer Otto von Kotzebue believed in 1816 that he had found a pathway through the waters of the North American Arctic and, while his claims were disputed, it stirred the British naval establishment into action. Encouraged by Sir John Barrow, the second secretary to the Admiralty, a new round of Arctic exploration began, but by then the field was an increasingly crowded one. The nineteenth century was abuzz with expeditions by European explorers and sailors, including Knud Rasmussen, John Ross, William Parry, Robert McClure and John Rae. Ships roamed up and down the North American Arctic hoping to discover a viable route through the Northwest Passage. Ice, first- and multi-year in age, blocked and crushed those ambitions and expeditions floundered. Some progress was possible overland with the help of sledge dogs and, when it was sought, advice from indigenous peoples living there. The first crossing of the Northwest Passage was not achieved until 1906, when the great Norwegian explorer Roald Amundsen successfully crossed in a converted herring fishing vessel.[11] These experiences helped

The Norwegian explorer Fridtjof Nansen and the ship *Fram* negotiating Arctic sea ice in May 1896.

nonetheless to add greatly to our collective descriptions of ice and snow.

Further south, Antarctic exploration received a boost after Captain James Cook's global voyages in the 1770s and 1780s took him as far south as the island of South Georgia. He may not have been the first to speculate about an immense ice-filled land further south. Polynesian oral histories speak of the seventh-century explorer Hui-Te-Rangiora sailing far south of New Zealand and encountering a 'white land'. But Cook was the first white European to record the southerly progress of his global expeditions. While doubtful about whether it might be possible to venture further due to sea ice and stormy weather, it did not deter others in the nineteenth century. British explorers such as James Weddell, spurred on by whalers and sealers eager to improve their commercially sensitive knowledge of sub-Antarctic islands such as South Shetlands, ventured further south to the waters off the Antarctic Peninsula. In 1820 the Russian explorer Fabian von Bellingshausen circumnavigated the Antarctic continent and sent a warning signal to the British that southern polar exploration was not going to be solely their purview. And to complicate matters still further, the French explorer Jules Dumont d'Urville was actively exploring the Antarctic in the late 1830s, and landed in 1840 on the shoreline of the continent.

Both north and south, the search and conquest of the poles was something quite different to tropical and temperate exploration. The rationale was less about commerce and more an exploratory 'first' that would inspire and inform domestic citizenry. Sponsoring governments and commercial companies were eager for kudos and attentive to the possibility of making a profit from sponsorship. While there had been speculation that an 'open polar sea' with great resource potential might await the first explorer, the drivers for the key protagonists involved in the 'race to the pole' were fame, money and pride. The ice and frozen sea covering the North Pole added to the sense of drama and excitement. In September 1909 the *New York Times* announced to its readers, 'Peary Discovers the North Pole After Eight Trials in 23 Years'.[12] On his return to Canada, the explorer

and adventurer Robert Peary claimed that he had reached the northernmost point in April of that year with his African American companion Matthew Henson. It was Peary's eighth and final attempt and it was not clear that anyone could have achieved what he alleged – a 37-day dash to the pole starting from northern Canada.

Jules Dumont d'Urville and the exploration of Adélie Territory, Antarctica, in January 1840 (painting by Louis Le Breton, who accompanied d'Urville on his expedition).

What made the achievement all the more remarkable was that another American polar explorer, Frederick Cook, claimed he had done so a year earlier in April 1908. Cook's claim was discredited, as he could not produce his navigational records. In the late 1980s it was revealed that Peary too might not have reached the furthest point north. In the expeditionary records, researchers began to cast doubt on his reported geographical position. Unlike the South Pole, the North Pole is harder to fix with a commemorative flag or cairn in the sense that it moves on floating ice. Britain's Wally Herbert, who successfully walked to the North Pole as part of the British Trans-Arctic Expedition (1968–9), was publicly sceptical of Peary's claims. Somewhere at the bottom of the central Arctic Ocean, there might reside an American flag placed in a tin that Peary claimed to have buried at the North Pole when he reached it in April 1909.[13] Maybe it is next to the Russian flag deposited there in August 2007.

The quest for the South Pole has also had its own dramas and controversies, as explorers such as Ernest Shackleton, Robert Scott and Roald Amundsen were involved in expeditions to reach the geographical heart of the Antarctic continent. The 1895 International Geographical Congress in London proved to be a powerful stimulant as leading establishment figures such as Sir Clements Markham of the Royal Geographical Society urged countries to launch a new round of expeditions to discover and explore the Antarctic. Belgian, Norwegian, British and American explorers and their sponsors supported a concerted programme of scientific investigation and overwintering exploration. After several adventurers, including Shackleton's privately organized 1907 Nimrod expedition, got within 110 km (70 miles) of the South Pole, Scott and Amundsen were involved in an infamous 'race to the pole', which saw Amundsen and his party reach the ultimate destination in December 1911. Ironically, Amundsen was supposed to be venturing towards the North Pole but changed his mind on hearing that Peary had apparently got there already. Scott and his Terra Nova party arrived second in January 1912 and on their return infamously perished close to their point of departure. For different reasons, both Amundsen and Scott became heroes in their respective countries, but the loss of Scott and his party was keenly felt, although the British polar establishment took comfort from the party's scientific collecting and their refusal to use dogs to help their progress over the ice.[14]

Scott's journals, which were published in 1913, represent one of the most eloquent if tragic accounts of what immense icescapes can do to the human body and mind. Over the course of the fateful expedition, the reader discovers how the cold and ice consumes accompanying Siberian ponies, causes injuries and ultimately consumes the final party. Captain Scott's last diary entry around March 1912 has a haunting simplicity, clearly written in the knowledge that survival was no longer possible: 'Had we lived, I should have a tale to tell of the hardihood, endurance and courage of my companions which would have stirred the heart of every Englishman. These rough notes and our dead bodies must tell the tale.'[15] These 'rough notes' narrate an extra-ordinary tale of polar blizzards, katabatic winds, starvation and surviving with an ever-diminishing number of companions.

The Australian explorer and geologist Douglas Mawson also allowed audiences to discover at third hand what ice, snow and wind could do to the human body and mind. His courage and endurance are the stuff of legend, including an experience in January 1913 where he found himself over 160 km (100 mi.) from the main base with little food left, no surviving dogs and no surviving companions. He faced imminent death. Remarkably, after struggling through blizzards he found a survival cairn laid by a rescue party and eventually made it back to base. As he later noted:

> For hours I lay in the bag, rolling over in my mind all that lay behind and the chance of the future. I seemed to stand alone on the wide shores of the world . . . My physical condition was such that I felt I might collapse at any moment . . . Several of my toes commenced to blacken and fester near the tips and the nails worked loose. There

Photograph of Robert Peary's sledge party as they 'reached' the North Pole in April 1909.

Roald Amundsen and party at the South Pole, 17 December 1911.

Douglas Mawson recovering after his miraculous escape from starvation and isolation. He was a member of the 1911–14 Australasian Antarctic Expedition.

appeared to be little hope . . . It was easy to sleep in the bag, and the weather was cruel outside.[16]

Later polar explorers have also discovered that the Antarctic is no place for the faint-hearted. Even if you survive, the legacies of such exposure to cold and ice could be devastating to the human body and mind.

Going deeper and wider

After the First World War, the commemoration of Scott and his party precipitated the establishment of the Scott Polar Research Institute at Cambridge University and renewed British interest in exploration and science in Antarctica. While heroism and polar exploration shifted in the twentieth century, as new technologies such as the aeroplane and mechanized transport enabled ever--increasing areas of the polar continent to be traversed, the lure of 'firsts' did not disappear. In 1957–8 Britain, Australia and New Zealand launched a Trans-Antarctic Expedition (TAE) led by Vivian Fuchs and Edmund Hillary, which took 99 days to cross the continent via the South Pole, with the aid of snow weasels and converted tractors. In the midst of the International Geo-physical Year (1957–8), the TAE on the face of it appeared to be a throwback to an earlier era of exploration.

By the late 1950s, it became clearer that further understanding would require more vertical rather than horizontal engagement. The new questions were how deep was the Antarctic ice sheet and what role did it perform in terms of shaping Earth's climate? What lay underneath the ice was the key question, not who would reach the South Pole first. As Fuchs and Hillary's book, *The Crossing of Antarctica*, noted, the TAE scientists involved in the expedition itself were conducting scientific experiments includ-ing measuring ice thickness throughout the journey. The two men, however, did not get on well with one another – Fuchs the scientist and Hillary the mountaineer were very different person-alities. But what made the TAE rather different to an earlier era was that time on the ice was now being measured in mere days.

For all the improvements in technology, clothing, geograph-ical knowledge and logistical support, it is still possible to perish there. The British explorer Henry Worsley died in January 2016 of exhaustion and dehydration. He was attempting to traverse nearly 1,500 km (930 mi.) over the polar continent in an attempt to reconstruct Ernest Shackleton's *Nimrod* expedition. Famously, Shackleton stopped some 150 km (93 mi.) from his ultimate des-tination because he sensed that any further would have made a

safe return less likely. After complaining of poor health some 50 km (31 mi.) short of his final destination, Worsley was airlifted to a hospital in Chile where he died of multiple organ failure. What killed Worsley was something that all polar explorers have had to cope with: dehydration. As he sweated, he became dehydrated and dangerously ill. In an environment surrounded by frozen water, many have died because of moisture loss made more dangerous by disorientation and even hallucination.

Tractors (Ferguson TE20) used by New Zealander Edmund Hillary in his transcontinental expedition across Antarctica in 1957.

Scaling heights and barriers

Altitude and latitude conspire to determine how far snow and ice extends over a mountain. The snow line varies considerably around the world. At the poles, snow and ice are found at sea level while in the European Alps 3,000 m (10,000 ft) above sea level would not be atypical. Distance from coastline can also make a difference in terms of precipitation and the degree to which snow converts to ice. When combined with seasonality, not all mountaineering and vertical exploration of the Earth involve encounters with ice and snow. However, high-altitude mountains are guaranteed to be ice covered, and present their own distinct exploratory challenges.

The history of summiting and mountaineering, while an integral part of humanity's migration over the Earth, developed a more formal history from the eighteenth century onwards with the inception of Alpinism. In 1760 the naturalist Horace Bénédict de Saussure offered a reward to anyone who was successful in climbing the highest mountain in France, Mont Blanc. Two local men, Jacques Balmant and Michel-Gabriel Paccard, claimed the reward when they reached the summit in August 1786. Saussure himself finally made it to the summit the following year with eighteen guides to help him. While at the top of the summit, Saussure performed the first scientific experiments, took barometric measurements and studied and recorded observations about high-altitude snow and ice. He published his findings in four volumes between 1779 and 1796 and established a scientific tradition of conducting research into high-altitude glaciology, biology, cartography, meteorology and geology. For Continental Europeans, such as the famous Swiss glaciologist Louis Agassiz, in the eighteenth and nineteenth centuries, exploration, mountaineering, nationalism and science informed one another.

Mountain exploration changed further with the onset of the British-led alpinist movement, where the motivation was not science but the pursuit of pleasure and enjoyment. An alpinist was someone who climbed the snow- and ice-covered mountains of the European Alps but in the British milieu it was a pastime for the privileged. Climbing over ice and snow was something for the social and political elites. By the 1850s, the British climber Sir Alfred Wills made mountaineering a fashionable pursuit, encouraging others to follow in his footsteps and tackle major mountains such as the Matterhorn. The Alpine Club acted as a gathering point for a generation of competitive climbers informed by professional debates about equipment, technique and the use of guides. Climbing the European Alps became increasingly competitive as British and German climbers sought to plant

their flags in mountain ice before their rivals. By the interwar period, mountaineering had taken on more sinister implications, as it became a platform for German nationalism and ideologies of Aryan masculinity.

Elsewhere, scaling the heights of North and South America became popular, with the Rockies attracting much interest from a new generation of proponents including Edwin James and John Fremont. In 1913 the highest peak in North America, Mount McKinley (now Denali), was summited and Canada's highest, Mount Logan, was conquered in 1925. Globally, the nineteenth century was a period of extraordinary achievement as mountaineers around the world scrambled and climbed their way to the top of the world's highest peaks, with the only exception being the highest mountain range in the world, the Himalayas. British climbers, however, were eager to change that. In 1924 George Mallory with his climbing partner Andrew Irvine set out to be the first to climb Mount Everest (8,848 m/29,000 ft). Having made the final camp, their ascent to the summit ended mysteriously. Mallory's body was eventually found in 1999, and even to this day it is not clear whether Mallory was returning from the summit or had died on the way up.

What mountaineers learned, often painfully, is that the high altitude environment is hazardous. By the time one has reached 8,000 m (26,000 ft), temperatures have dropped steadily by about 10°C (50°F) for every 1,000 m (3,300 ft) ascended. High winds, freezing temperatures and entry into the 'death zone' are part of the grim reality to be embraced by the intrepid. At 8,000 m oxygen levels are so low that human life becomes difficult to sustain. Swiss doctor Edouard Wyss-Dunant identified this phenomenon in 1953, the same year that Hillary and Tenzing stood triumphantly and briefly on top of Everest. As generations of mountaineers have recorded, once you pass beyond 8,000 m you enter the 'death zone' and any chance of survival necessitates descent.

Even for those who survive the 'death zone', the ice, wind and cold could take a terrible toll on the human body. In June 1950 Maurice Herzog and Louis Lachenal became the first people to

Gustave Doré's print of the first ascent of the Matterhorn, by the British mountaineer Edward Whymper and his party in 1865.

climb a mountain over 8,000 m high. They reached the summit of Mount Annapurna 1 in the Himalayas, the tenth highest mountain in the world, at the first attempt. But it was eventful. Equipment was lost and the party left exposed to freezing temperatures, resulting in the loss of all toes and most fingers to frostbite. In his classic account of their ascent, Herzog reflected on the dilemma facing all mountaineers as they approach the 'death zone': should they continue or go back?

> In an hour or two, perhaps, victory would be ours. Must we give up? Impossible! My whole being revolted against the idea. I had made up my mind, irrevocably. Today we were consecrating an ideal, and no sacrifice was too great. I heard my voice clearly: 'I should go on by myself.'[17]

The men decided to push to the summit. Despite the risks and loss of limbs, they made it and returned alive. Lachenal later lost his life in a climbing accident in France in 1955 and Herzog went

North face of the Annapurna massif, Himalayas.

on to become a French minister of sport and culture and mayor of the mountain resort of Chamonix.

But it was not just men who were pushing themselves into the 'death zones' of the world's mountains; women were also scaling great heights and, in so doing, exploring the highest points on Earth. One of the greatest mountaineers was the Frenchwoman Claude Kogan, who was the first to climb the 7,000-m (23,000-ft) Mount Nun in the Himalayas in 1953, and was at one stage described as the 'highest woman in the world'.[18] She later died in an avalanche while leading an all-female expedition aiming to climb the world's sixth-highest mountain, the 8,200-m (27,000-ft) Cho Oyu in Tibet, in 1959. Before her untimely death, she had climbed an array of mountains in Europe and South America and helped to dislodge the dominant masculine culture that surrounded high-altitude mountaineering. As the anthropologist Sherry Ortner reflected in her book, *Life and Death on Mount Everest*:

Sherpa Tenzing Norgay with Edmund Hillary on the slope of Everest (photograph taken by John Henderson – John, a tea planter in Darjeeling, and his wife Jill, the secretary of the mountain club, were involved with the Sherpas and the provisioning of the various climbs).

Himalayan mountaineering until the 1970s had been an overwhelmingly male sport. It was engaged in almost (but not quite) exclusively by men, both Sherpa and 'first world': it built on male styles of interaction derived from other all-male institutions, especially after the army; and while it was about many things – nature and nation, materiality and spirituality, the moral quality of the inner self, and the meaning of life – it was always in part about masculinity and manhood.[19]

While mountain climbing and polar exploration remain danger-ous, our attitude towards mountains and the snow and ice that top them is much changed from hundreds of years ago. Women climbers are now well established and respected within the sport of mountaineering and climbing. And there is now greater appreciation of the 'hidden histories' of mountaineering, includ-ing the role of Sherpas, among them the world-famous Tenzing Norgay, and the contribution their detailed knowledge and experience of mountain environments made to climbers around the world.

The first woman to climb Everest was a Japanese climber, Junko Tabei in May 1975. Eager to challenge gender discrimination in Japan, Tabei pioneered all-women climbing expeditions. In 1969, she established the Joshi-Taban climbing club and led an expedition to the Himalayas in 1970. Famed for her endurance and determination, her ascent of Annapurna III was notable because she coped with heavy snowfall, freezing temperatures and high winds. The Everest ascent was notable because there was little sponsorship, coupled with domestic opposition to her high-profile climbing endeavours. It was beset by an avalanche of such severity that she had to crawl to the top of the mountain.

The first women at the South Pole arrived in November 1969, five months after men landed on the moon. Again they faced similar expression of opposition to female climbers to that experienced by Tabei. The u.s. Navy and civilian operators such as British Antarctic Survey were reluctant to embrace female participation, fearing that their presence might disrupt the everyday routines of research base life. Other excuses for non-participation included the notions that women were incapable of coping with the vagaries of ice and cold, and that they would demand separate bath and toilet facilities. The inaugural party of 1969 included a New Zealander called Pamela Young, who was working at the time as a field assistant, a group of American female scientists – Lois Jones, Terry Lee Tickhill Terrell, Eileen McSaveney and Kay Lindsay – as well as a journalist called Jean Pearson. Since 1969, women have been a near constant presence in many Antarctic science and logistical programmes.

A u.s.-led initiative called Girls on Ice is one example of how girls and women are being encouraged to think about science careers involving ice and snow. Supported by the University of Alaska, it aims to promote glaciology and mountaineering to young women, and in 2016 two expeditions were launched in the mountains of Alaska and Washington State. Professional organizations such as the Association for Early Career Polar Scientists are also helping to 'open up' the Arctic and Antarctic for future generations of female researchers. The current director of the British Antarctic Survey is Professor Jane Francis, the first

Junko Tabei, the first woman to climb Everest, in 1975.

woman to lead an organization that can trace its roots back to the Second World War.

Discovering yet more ice

High-altitude, interstellar and subterranean exploring continue to intersect with one another, leading to further discoveries of ice and what might lie beneath it. With the assistance of satellite remote sensing and aerial radio-echo sounding techniques,

Dr Jerri Nielsen, who famously treated her breast cancer while stationed at the South Pole research station in 1998–9.

scientists discovered a vast mountain range hidden under the Antarctic ice sheet. With jagged peaks estimated to be up to 2,500 m (8,200 ft) in height and 1,200 km (750 mi.) in length, the Gamburtsev Mountains are being explored in a rather more remote way than high-altitude human pioneers.[20] A recent NASA airborne radar mission in Greenland revealed new understandings of the hidden landscapes covered by ice and snow. Under what was termed Operation Ice Bridge, NASA and researchers from Germany and the United Kingdom used advanced radar system technology to penetrate through vast areas of ice in order to measure the bedrock below. Underneath central Greenland lies a vast canyon, larger than the Grand Canyon, filled with ice but a conduit for subglacial meltwater from the centre to the coastline. As the Greenland ice melts, long-term monitoring of the canyon will provide important clues to the future stability of the ice sheet.

With the development of interstellar technology, we continue to make further discoveries of ice. Thanks to long-range roving missions by agencies such as NASA and the European Space Agency (ESA), we know that ice is found throughout the solar system and that its presence is instrumental in shaping planetary systems. Icy moons, comets and asteroids are integral to where ice is found. Space scientists argue that the distribution of water and ice in the solar system offers insights into how planets and moons were created some 4 billion years ago. Planets and bodies furthest away from the Sun were sufficiently cool for water to condense and collect. Comets may have been responsible for transporting water around the solar system. And the creation of Jupiter, the earliest planet to be created, might have been possible because of the presence of water and ice which allowed dust and gas to condense into a substantial and relatively stable mass.

There is no reason to think that we will not make further discoveries of ice throughout the solar system and perhaps these will act as an imaginative counter-weight to ongoing stories about earthly losses.

3 Imagining and Representing Ice

My love is like to ice, and I to fire:
How comes it then that this her cold so great
Is not dissolved through my so hot desire,
But harder grows the more I her entreat?

Or how comes it that my exceeding heat
Is not allayed by her heart-frozen cold,
But that I burn much more in boiling sweat,
And feel my flames augmented manifold?

What more miraculous thing may be told,
That fire, which all things melts, should harden ice,
And ice, which is congeal'd with senseless cold,
Should kindle fire by wonderful device?

Such is the power of love in gentle mind,
That it can alter all the course of kind.
Edmund Spenser, 'Ice and Fire', 1590

To trace the human encounter with ice is to enter a world filled with cultural, folkloric, mythical, scientific and spiritual qualities. As we have noted, some of the most advanced science and technology has been integral to the discovery of ice on distant planets, moons, comets and asteroids. Closer to home, ice has been respected and revered by indigenous peoples for centuries

Inuksuit are human-made stone monuments that were (and still are) used as navigation aids and food caches for the native peoples who travelled all over the Arctic region.

and features strongly in oral cultures around the Arctic region. Ice was part and parcel of a world in the making – where its presence allowed communities to travel, to hunt, to meet up and socialize, and to trade with others within and beyond the high latitudes. The temporary Bering Land Bridge enabled exploration and colonization of the Americas, and large areas of glaciation ensured that sea level was some 90 m (300 ft) lower 20,000 years ago.[1] Rising sea levels effectively separated Asia from North America, and created distinct geographical and genetic patterns of human communities.

High and cold places are intimately connected to the imaginative, even the spiritual.[2] Up and above the cloud line, mountains offered a sort of transcendence from earthly concerns and the white landscapes of Alpine, Arctic and Antarctic environments provoked in the Western Romantic traditions an appeal to the sublime. This referred to how the explorer's body and mind was moved by an overwhelming sense of awe, humility and even terror in the face of such physical immensity. In Christianity, the association with transcendence, height and spiritual power is well established, and was in itself a vital element in the eighteenth- and nineteenth-century evocations of the sublime. There is, however, a pictorial tradition of winter landscapes in Europe from the sixteenth century onwards that was low-lying and vernacular, especially in Holland.[3] Later, as the sublime aesthetic became more prominent, the icy peaks of the European Alps and polar regions were protuberant.

In Western aesthetics and literature, we can identify two traditions of the sublime with relevance to ice and the elemental geographies of the Earth. Edmund Burke's *A Philosophical Enquiry into the Origin of Our Ideas of the Sublime and Beautiful* (1757) made a distinction between beauty and the sublime, with consequences for how we feel and react to objects and landscapes. We might marvel at the delicacy of a snowflake while a glacier or iceberg might overwhelm us. The size, scale and volume of ice provoke a sense of awe, wonder and even terror as we confront something that can overwhelm us. The untamed power of the world was something to marvel at but also to fear.

Pieter Bruegel the Younger, *Winter Landscape with a Bird Trap*, 1620s, oil on panel.

Immanuel Kant's *Observations on the Feeling of the Beautiful and Sublime* (1776) and *The Critique of Judgement* (1790) consider how the sublime identifies those experiences (for example, storms) and structures (such as ice-covered mountains) that threaten to overwhelm us. In his rendition of the sublime, Kant posits the view that there might be a mathematical sublime (things that are genuinely enormous compared to us) and the dynamical sublime (which threatens to overwhelm our powers of reason). For Kant, our pleasure in nature is tempered by our power of reason to transcend something that might appear to be overwhelming.

For much of the twentieth century, a combination of geophysics and geopolitics transformed the world's icy regions and fed a human desire for mastery over the ice. Vast sums of money were spent collecting data about ice on land, at sea and via space. In the twenty-first century, we are more likely to think of cold places as indicative of rapid global climate change and planetary vulnerability. Data collection is being put to work to reconstruct past climates and search for signs of possible futures. We are now more likely to express darker aesthetic appreciations of ice as we are forced to confront the spectre of a world with less ice.[4] As with snow layers laid down on a glacier, our encounters and experiences are subject to accumulation, compaction and disruption.

The language and imagery used to describe snow and ice has become somewhat uglier, as we are forced to engage with melting, loss, vanishing and disappearance to describe our realities. The revival of Gothic and horror aesthetic and literary conventions reveals clues as to how artists, film-makers, scientists and novelists are confronting the dark, malevolent forces of unnatural levels of warming, which asks of us profound questions about the implications for us, for the natural world and for a future world of 'inhuman ecologies'.

Ice and popular culture

Cold, frost, ice and snow are everyday realities for many people, and their omnipresence has etched itself into popular culture, including Robert Frost and Wallace Steven's beguiling poetry, ice and snow festivals, winter sports and leisure, television shows such as *Game of Thrones*, films such as the children's *Ice Age* trilogy, mountainous novels such as H. P. Lovecraft's fantastical *At the Mountains of Madness* (1936), Marvel superheroes such as Captain Cold and Iceman, and winter landscape art. Ice, frost and snow have animated the spiritual and religious registers of life and, over millennia, pagan faiths, mythologies and folklores. Organized religions have paid careful attention to how the intersection of light, darkness, ice and fire created the world. In Norse mythology, ice and fire were integral to Norse cosmology and one of the nine kingdoms, namely Niflheim, was populated with glaciers, river ice and cold mists. The first men and women to populate the Earth owe their origins to the creation of a Norse god called Ymir, who emerged out of melting glacial ice. Ymir's early existence was made possible by a cow that survived by licking blocks of salty, glacial ice. The cow in turn provided Ymir with milk. Every Icelandic child, growing up in a country where ice, fire, cold and heat intermingle with one another, grows up learning about Ymir and the Norse creation myth.[5]

In Canada, one could point to the evocative early to mid-twentieth-century art deco paintings of icebergs, glaciers, snow-covered mountains and frozen lakes by Lawren Harris;

the poetry of Robert Service such as 'The Cremation of Sam McGee' (1907); Inuit legends about ice, snow and iconic animals such as the Snow Owl (the Ookpik); the annual Jack Frost Children's Winterfest (Jack Frost was a comic superhero who could create ice and generate cold); and a rich tradition of French-, English-, and Inuit-language movies such *La Guerre des Tuques* (1984), *Atanarjuat: The Fast Runner* (2001), *The Snow Walker* (2003) and *Arctic Defenders* (2013). The Quebecois poet and singer-songwriter Gilles Vigneault famously claimed in his well-known 1964 song 'Mon Pays' that his country was epitomized by winter. Margaret Atwood thought the mythologies and stories told about the Canadian North were symptomatic of *Strange Things*.[6] Atwood draws attention to a white settler Canadian fascination with the charm and menace of the Canadian north.

In Russia, it is difficult to underestimate the role of ice, snow and the long winter as it grips the country for many months. Russia's cold climate has played a significant role in shaping its

A painting of 1790 by the Danish artist Nicolai Abildgaard, depicting Ymir suckling the cow Auðumbla.

geopolitical history, as several invading forces have been repelled because of the cold and ice. The invasion by Napoleon in 1812 failed to conquer Russia despite taking an army of 600,000 eastwards. Severe frosts and snow were blamed for restricting mobility, exposing troops to frostbite and undermining their morale. The Nazi invasion in 1941 floundered not only because of stubborn Russian resistance, but because senior military planners failed to anticipate the possibility of extended winter warfare. While Soviet historians were eager to lionize the heroism of the Russian/Soviet soldier, they were paradoxically less willing to acknowledge the role of cold and ice in helping to protect Russia and isolate and weaken those unfortunate enough to be imprisoned in remote and cold labour camps (Gulags) in Siberia/the Soviet Far East.[7]

The long Russian winter has also bequeathed us a rich literary and visual tradition of representing ice and snow in myriad

Constantinovich Aivazovsky, *Winter Scene in Little Russia*, 1868, oil on canvas.

ways: simply as cold but also evoking the gamut of human emotions and conditions including hunger, grief, beauty, happiness, clarity and wonder. Alexander Pushkin's beautiful poem 'Winter Morning' invokes the beguiling qualities of a wintry landscape:

> The snow below the bluish skies
> Like a majestic carpet lies,
> And in the light of day it shimmers
> The woods are dusky. Through the frost
> The greenish fir-trees are exposed;
> And under ice, a river glitters.[8]

By contrast, the haunting verses of *Winter Sonnets* by another Russian poet, Vyacheslav Ivanov, use the analogy of ice and snow to speak of the 1917 Revolution as being akin to the elemental, unleashing brutal forces archetypical of a Russian winter where the perils of cold, privation and hunger take their toll. His

Vasily Vasilyevich Vereshchagin, *Napoleon's Retreat from Moscow*, 19th century, oil painting.

despair and unease are made worse by anxiety about the health and welfare of his family in the aftermath of Revolution.[9]

There is also a transnational sharing economy at work when it comes to legends, rituals and fairy tales involving ice and snow. Father Christmas, winter solstice festivals, the Abominable Snowman/Yeti and Father/Jack Frost are not exclusive to any one country or region. In Korea, Father Frost might be described as Santa Kullosu or Santa Grandfather in a country that also follows other East Asian cultures in celebrating winter festivals, including the solstice on 21 and 22 December. In China, it is known as the Dongzhi Festival and special festive foods are shared within families. In the United States, Disneyland adopted the Yeti as part of their Matterhorn Bobsled ride, while the Belgian writer Hergé imagined the Yeti to be something less formidable than might have been expected in *Tintin in Tibet* (1960). In the Japanese Pokémon game series, the Yeti was

Ice rink at Seoul City Hall, Korea.

reimagined as Abomasnow, an ice monster capable of invoking fierce blizzards and hailstorms. With its origins in German and Norse folklore legends, the mythical Jack Frost embodies frost, ice and snow and is thought to be responsible for frostbite and the frosting of windows in older houses. Over time, he has been imagined as a superhero, villain and even a protagonist in the nineteenth-century American Civil War.[10]

In Britain, informed by a Judaeo-Christian heritage, the association between snow, ice and Christmas is pronounced. Every year, speculation is rife about whether there will be a 'white Christmas' and families settle down to watch popular television shows such as *The Snowman*, a story of a snowman who takes a little boy to see Father Christmas. While passages of the Bible speak of ice and snow (such as in the books of Job, Psalms and Revelation), it is not associated with the birth of Jesus. Prior to the spread of Christianity, the winter solstice around 22 December was celebrated by Alpine communities. One of Austria's oldest midwinter folk rituals, the Perchtenlauf, takes place in early January when young men dressed in white costumes and masks wave birch and fir twigs (and nowadays jangle cowbells) to ward off evil spirits in the hope of inducing a mild spring and warm summer. Their aim is to herald a prosperous harvest and good fortune.

While snow and ice are not uncommon in the Holy Land, the link to Christmas owes more to a Victorian-era invention of tradition, which coincided with the hosting of winter fairs, the purchasing of Christmas cards and trees, and unseasonably cold spells of weather associated with the tail end of the 'Little Ice Age'. Charles Dickens's morality tale, *A Christmas Carol*, published in 1843, brought the trinity of snow, cold and Christmas together in the popular Victorian imagination. Dickens's collaboration with playwright and storyteller Wilkie Collins on the play about the lost Franklin expedition, 'The Frozen Deep', might well have inspired his interest in snow, cold and the human condition. In the story of Ebenezer Scrooge and the Three Ghosts of Christmas, Dickens explores the social geographies of London with Scrooge and others as representative of an everyday life punctuated by inequality and harshness. As Dickens wrote of Scrooge, 'No wind that blew was bitterer than he, no falling snow was more intent upon its purpose, no pelting rain less open to entreaty.' The haunting presence of former business partner Jacob Marley and the Three Ghosts eventually softens Scrooge's demeanour, leading him to act as the living embodiment of a Christmas characterized by generosity and compassion.

Present-day children, however, are far more likely to know the animated Disney film *Frozen* (2013) than Dickens's famous Christmas tale. Loosely based on Hans Christian Andersen's 1844 tale 'The Snow Queen', the film was a commercial hit throughout North America, Europe and East Asia. Its cast of characters include an ice cutter (Kristoff), a reindeer (Sven), a snowman (Olaf), and sisters Anna and Elsa, princesses of a (fictional) northern kingdom, Arandelle. Elsa possesses a special and dangerous power – she can turn things and people into ice. Usually hidden and controlled by wearing purple gloves, Elsa accidentally hits Anna in the heart with her special freezing power, gradually turning Anna to ice throughout the latter part of the film. As the evil Hans tries to kill Elsa with a sword stroke, Anna jumps in front to save her. At that exact moment Anna's freezing process coincidentally completes. Hans hits his sword on her ice body and is thwarted. However, because this is an act of love (for her sister rather than, as expected, an act of romantic love), the curse is broken and Anna thaws. Due to her state-change, Anna prevents Elsa's death.

As a fairy-tale archetype, the Ice or Snow Queen is inevitably gendered and characterized as a troubled, difficult, petulant, evil and socially isolated woman.[11] She is a sociopath and thus some of the claims about the film exhibiting a progressive gender politics seem misplaced. In *Frozen*, Elsa as a Snow Queen is distressed by her special power (akin to a 'freezer of hearts') and yet struggles to control a 'frosty' demeanour, which is rarely welcoming. She is accused in the film of being a monster by Prince Hans because she will not give her approval for the wedding to Anna. Unmarried, she is represented as dismissive of eligible men and indifferent to the feelings of others, bar her sister Anna. As part of their odyssey, Anna and Kristoff begin to unravel the true character of Elsa – she is vulnerable, sad and deeply hurt by the sudden and unexpected loss of their parents. Anna is only able to traverse the ice and snow with the expert guidance of Kristoff. Ice in *Frozen* proves stubbornly gendered, and circumscribes the ability of the two young women to act independently of others.

Ice and Romantic Europeans

Eighteenth- and nineteenth-century explorers, novelists and travellers to the Arctic, Antarctic and European mountain ranges were eager to understand, engage with and represent ice and snow. Literary and visual cultures found ice to be commercially and aesthetically alluring. It was both a literary/visual and financial source to be harvested like Arctic and Antarctic fish, seals and whales. It was also a place to experiment. Not everyone who visited (or imagined visiting) the ice-filled worlds of the North Atlantic and the Arctic region was searching for the Northwest Passage or intent on extracting commercial profit from its seas and landscapes.

The English Romantic poet Samuel Taylor Coleridge embodies strongly the power of ice and snow to beguile. While attending Christ's Hospital School in West Sussex, he was taught by William Wales, an astronomer who served on Captain James Cook's *Resolution*.[12] Wales would have been well placed to convey the excitement and drama of ice-filled seas and the search for worlds beyond the conventional scope of the global map. Coleridge's epic poems 'The Rime of the Ancient Mariner' and 'Frost at Midnight' articulate the scope for ice, frost and snow to inspire, terrorize and probe the divine origins of the world. For Coleridge, inspired by pantheism, the ice acts as a 'polar spirit', a supernatural entity not tied to one particular religious denomination. In 'Rime of the Ancient Mariner', ice and rime cracks, growls, roars and howls. But in his 'Destiny of Nations', the ice plays a different role, this time being enrolled

in an imagination of the Arctic as a place of political and intellectual freedom, a world far removed from stifling European cultures and societies.[13]

Frederick Church, *The Icebergs*, 1861, oil on canvas.

Utilizing the aesthetics of the polar sublime, novelists such as Mary Shelley (in *Frankenstein*, 1818) and later Victorian painters such as Edwin Landseer imagine a world where ice and snow are strange and often complicit with alienation and the idea of the monstrous. Shelley's account is of a man, Victor Frankenstein, who thinks he can control a monster that he has created in his laboratory. He narrates his tale of experimentation to a ship captain and Arctic explorer, Robert Walton. Inspired by the poetry of Coleridge, Shelley articulates a vision of a frozen Arctic that is in the grip of ice, snow, fog and darkness. Walton's ship is trapped in Arctic sea ice, where the monster is well adapted. Frankenstein knows this because of an earlier encounter with the monster on the Mer de Glace (Sea of Ice) in the European Alps. As the monster taunts Frankenstein: 'My reign is not yet over – you live, and my power is complete. Follow me; I seek the everlasting ices of the north, where you will feel the misery of cold and frost, to which I am impassive.'[14] As the reader discovers, the creature, overcome by both remorse and regret for the eventual death of his creator, Victor, drifts

Engraving by Gustave Doré for an 1876 edition of Samuel Taylor Coleridge's 1798 poem 'The Rime of the Ancient Mariner'.

away in darkness to a fate unknown. Shelley invites the reader to find the dangers of masculine hubris in both Frankenstein's experimentation and Walton's exploration.

Shelley's novel was published at a time of growing interest in the exploits of Arctic explorers and their tales of monstrous seas, ice and weather that battered ships and their passengers and unsettled the human senses.[15] Ice was monstrous, beautiful and baffling. It was also inviting. In *Frankenstein*, Captain Walton is driven by his quest for the North Pole because he believes that an 'open polar sea' lies beyond the pack ice. It was in his words 'a region of beauty and delight' and contemporary explorers and geographers imagined it to be benign, resourceful and just reward for their tribulations. Romantic writers, artists and poets were helping to assemble a view of ice not as blank and beyond representation but as something capable of generating insights about the human condition and its imaginative possibilities.

Film poster for *Frankenstein* (1931).

As Joseph Conrad (who had sailed through sub-Antarctic waters) wrote in his novella *Falk* (1901), the ice could also eviscerate codes of morality as men simply struggled to survive. After fighting the remaining men on a doomed ship circulating aimlessly in Antarctic waters, the protagonist Falk is able to declare: 'They all died . . . But I would not die . . . Only the best man would survive. It was a great, terrible, and cruel misfortune.'[16] Writing in the aftermath of the lost Franklin expedition of 1845 and the infamous Greely expedition, Conrad caught a public mood of despondency. If the Franklin affair shocked British audiences, then Greely perturbed the American public. Greely's party became lost and dangerously close to death while seeking refuge on Cape Sabine in the Canadian Arctic. By the time they were rescued in June 1884, only six men had endured from a party of 25, and at least one was executed on Greely's command because he stood accused of stealing food. Later, it emerged that the surviving six might have resorted to cannibalism in order to stay alive prior to their rescue. So the capacity of ice to invoke hunger and desperation in white European and North American men was already widely publicized and stood in contrast to those who would venerate them as heroes. Conrad's novel captured something of a more sceptical zeitgeist about the civilizational element of polar exploration. Could ice provoke cannibalism in men?[17]

Indigenous peoples and their ice worlds

Encounters with Arctic ice in the nineteenth century were all the more intriguing because the worlds in which European explorers found themselves were quite different to those of the Antarctic and high mountains. The Arctic was and is an inhabited space. Inhabitants include the Inupiat, Yup'ik, Alutiiq, Aleuts and Athapaskans of Alaska; the Inuit, Inuvialuit and Dene of northern Canada; the Kalaallit and Inughuit of Greenland; the Saami of Fennoscandia and Russia's Kola peninsula; and the Chukchi, Even, Evenk, Nenets, Nivkhi and Yukaghir of the Russian Far North and Siberia. There are around 300,000 indigenous peoples in the total population of about 4 million who live north of the Arctic Circle.

Indigenous peoples have held and continue to hold a complex repertoire of stories, mythologies and beliefs pertaining to the Arctic, including its ice, snow and water. While many indigenous peoples may have adopted Christianity following waves of European and American colonial encounters, Inuit and other indigenous cultures continued to be shaped by beliefs that inanimate objects, animals and plant life possess spiritual properties and that there is no rigid distinction between the spiritual and physical worlds. Inuit belief systems were literally rooted in the unpredictability and environmental extremes encountered in the Arctic, and often operated as a warning system to community members about living cautiously and respectfully in their surroundings. Within Inuit communities, elders and shamans in particular were critical in ensuring that social rituals including taboos were respected, and warned of the perilous consequences if the spirits were disrespected.

Inuit cultures were for millennia oral cultures and storytelling was elemental to the reproduction of culture and belief systems. Stories coupled with songs and dance and material objects such as carvings were part of a broader repertoire of performance-based and material cultures, which addressed the here and now and the afterlife. All stories reinforce the importance of living respectfully with non-human communities and the intersecting physical and spiritual worlds. Inuit myths are animated by legends of extraordinary characters such as Sedna, the sea goddess, held to be responsible for the fate of marine mammals living in the oceans. As a culture dependent on hunting whales, fish and seals, appeasing Sedna was considered vital to the long-term survival of local communities. Other figures such as Kiviuk helped to account for the presence of fish in the Arctic and the absence of trees on the tundra.[18]

For Inuit, the dangers posed by the ice, sea and ever-changing weather also sustained myths that emphasized the Arctic as highly dangerous and filled with terrifying demons and chameleon-like characters that change from animal to animal. In some accounts, suspicious characters exist that are rarely seen but are capable of luring children into the sea or simply capturing and killing unwary humans. For those who violated taboos, the role of the shaman was judged to be critical in enabling redemption and forgiveness. In one example involving Sedna, the shaman entered into the ocean in order to thwart Sedna's hair from becoming entangled with marine mammals which was preventing hunters from securing vital food supplies. The shaman disentangles her hair so that the animals can be freed again, which was vital for small and highly isolated communities.

Moving onshore, Inuit and indigenous belief also shaped the imagination of the interior in Greenland. The inland region was

Illustration of
an Inuit village,
Oopungnewing,
near Frobisher Bay
on Baffin Island,
c. 1865.

a space of extreme and excess, filled with monsters, ghosts and marginal communities trapped by the ice.[19] Very few journeyed into the interior. Mountain peaks were regarded as dangerous in western Greenlandic culture, which was rooted more in marine activities such as fishing and sealing. Venturing inland was a seasonal affair, reserved for the short summer, and unusual for communities that looked outwards rather than inwards. Culturally, it was a risky space, where it was easy to imagine dread and terror. The Inuit hero-figure was someone who could enter the inland ice kingdom and overcome the dangers posed by animal monsters, giant humans and dog-people who lay in wait for the brave and foolish. Ancient Greeks might have recognized the Greenland interior as functioning as a kind of elaborate labyrinth, where vicious mythical creatures waited for the unfortunate. If the Greeks had Theseus as the slayer of the Minotaur, Inuit have their heroes, including the wandering Kiviuq who faced off bears, giants, cannibals, spirits and sea monsters.

The Saint Elias Mountains are situated at the intersection of Alaska and British Columbia and Yukon in Canada. The anthropologist Julie Cruikshank considers how native populations, the Athapaskans and Tlingit, understood glaciers in rather different ways to European and North American explorers and travellers.[20] For those who lived there, rather than those who travelled there, the glaciers represented 'permeable boundaries' between the human and the more than human. The ice that occupied and travelled through and over the mountainous landscapes was a living, moving force capable of agency, and senses including hearing and smell. Mindful of overdetermining a sharp distinction between native and non-native understandings of glaciers, Cruickshank looks to the oral accounts of the glaciers to better understand how they were thought to be capable of responding to human action and impropriety. The glaciers are imagined in native animist cosmologies as living bodies co-existing in a world where it is considered foolish to 'offend' glaciers.

Ice and the sublime

When it comes to the imagination and representation of ice and snow, the power of the sublime and its enduring legacy cannot be underestimated. Ice embodied and reflected the spirit of the sublime. Yoked with a period encompassing the 1750s to the 1850s, a string of artists, poets and writers and their critics developed new aesthetic codes and representations of ice and mountains and the elemental forces and extraordinary scales that threatened to overwhelm the human presence.[21] Painters such as J.M.W. Turner, and his encounters with the ice-capped Alps, and poets such as Percy Bysshe Shelley, who mused about snow-covered Alpine landscapes, are some of the best-known examples of the period. For artists and poets, the ice could be instilled with a sense of greatness but also rendered pleasurable because the viewer and reader were safely removed from its elemental forces and qualities. The sublime was inspired and informed by philosophical interventions as well. As we have noted, Edmund Burke's *A Philosophical Enquiry into the Origin of Our Ideas of the Sublime and Beautiful* (1757) helped to frame our understandings of nature, including ice and mountains. As he argued,

Casper David Friedrich, *The Sea of Ice*, 1824, oil on canvas.

Whatever is fitted in any sort to excite the idea of pain, and danger, that is to say, whatever is in any sort terrible, or is [indeed] conversant about terrible objects, or operates in a manner analogous to terror, is a source of the *sublime*; that is, it is productive of the strongest emotion which the mind is capable of feeling.[22]

Caspar David Friedrich's painting *The Sea of Ice* (1824) provides a popular entrée into the ice sublime. Informed by his imagination and first-hand observations of ice on the River Elbe, Friedrich never visited the Arctic. The picture was a product of his imagination. Jagged ice blocks, carelessly overlaid with one another and pointing towards the sky, overwhelm the observer. When you look a little more closely, however, there is the outline of a ship's hull entrapped in this sea of ice: an object of mobility immobilized by a material that will not release its grip until a combination of ocean currents, warming

winds and rising temperatures have combined to loosen it. For later generations of sailors seeking passage through the Arctic sea ice, Friedrich's picture stood as a stark warning as to what they might confront.[23]

John Brett,
Glacier of Rosenlaui,
1856, oil on canvas.

One of the most interesting examples of the ice sublime is John Brett's depiction of the *Glacier of Rosenlaui* in 1856. A British-born landscape painter, Brett visited Switzerland and was inspired by Victorian artists and art critics such as John William Inchbold and John Ruskin. Fascinated by the geology and biology of landscapes, and inspired by Ruskin's 'Of Mountain Beauty', he spent a summer in central Switzerland at the small village of Rosenlaui. He met Inchbold while in Switzerland and his painting of the *Glacier of Rosenlaui* faithfully reproduces his fascination for the geological qualities of places and in this case the intersection between ice and rock. In this beautiful painting, the eye is initially drawn to the foregrounded boulders and stones that are depicted with great care and attention. What lies behind the boulders, however, is the icy mass of the glacier waiting to devour those exposed rock formations. Reminiscent of a raging river, the ice appears ready and willing to continue its descent from above to envelope rather than retreat from those exposed boulders. One gets a profound sense here that what is being painted is something raw and untrammelled by human intervention as the rocks and boulders bear witness to the capacity of ice to smooth, smother and striate the underlying geology of place.[24]

The role of the human is integral to the sublime and its relationship with ice. The Victorian painter Edwin Landseer dramatically captured the invocation of the sublime as overwhelming – even terrifying. In a painting that hangs at my university, Royal Holloway, *Man Proposes, God Disposes*, Landseer offers up a thoroughly dystopian vision of ice and the Arctic. In his depiction of the ill-fated expedition led by Sir John Franklin

Edwin Landseer, *Man Proposes, God Disposes*, 1864, oil on canvas.

to find the Northwest Passage, the Arctic is a cruel wasteland dominated by marauding polar bears intent on satisfying their hunger. A wrecked ship, a torn flag and human remains consolidate a sense of desperation and of sheer horror. Painting in 1864, Landseer was working against the backdrop of febrile searching for the Franklin expedition members amid rumours that surviving crew had resorted to cannibalism in order to survive the icy and cold conditions they found themselves in. The search for the Northwest Passage, while considered to be commercially compelling, might, as Landseer's depiction suggested, actually be a fool's errand.[25] Every summer time, the painting is covered in order to allay student fears about the curse of Franklin falling upon them as they take their exams in the Picture Gallery.

Disastrous icebergs

The sinking of the RMS *Titanic* in April 1912 remains evocative. It was a disastrous maiden voyage but it was not the first iceberg disaster.[26] In the nineteenth century, a number of vessels had been beset by disaster. In May 1849, the SS *Maria* collided with an iceberg close to the Canadian coastline. The vessel had picked up emigrants from Limerick with the intended destination being Quebec City. Remarkably, twelve people survived out of 121 because they either were able to seek sanctuary with a nearby boat or clung to ice and survived long enough to be rescued. The earliest losses were from the 1820s, where icebergs sunk the SS *Mount-stone* and SS *Superb* off the coastline of Newfoundland. What is notable about so many of the shipping-based disasters is that they occurred off the eastern North American coastline.

The popular term 'iceberg alley' refers to the physical geography phenomenon of ice being funnelled down from northern Greenland to Newfoundland via the Davis Strait. Many of the icebergs spotted off the Canadian coastline in places like Newfoundland owe their point of origin to west Greenlandic glaciers. Compounding things still further, dense fog makes navigation even more dangerous as warmer waters from the south come into contact with cold northern currents. All of which was to prove disastrous for the largest passenger ship in the world at the time of its sailing. Over 1,500 lives were lost when the RMS *Titanic* collided with icebergs. Seven hundred passengers survived due to calm if cold seas and the vicinity of the SS *Carpathia*, which rescued them and took them to their intended destination of New York. The captain of the *Carpathia* later reported that the surrounding sea was filled with sea ice, including icebergs estimated to be hundreds of feet high.

The sinking of the *Titanic*, rather than earlier iceberg-related disasters, generated huge outpourings of public anguish and shock, and until the onset of the First World War dominated English-language cultural conversations. The death toll was nine to ten times higher than a previous accident. Poets, novelists and painters all offered their interpretations of the event itself. For some it was a moment of divine judgement: literally an act

RMS *Titanic* leaving Southampton on its inaugural voyage to New York, April 1912.

of God determined to remind humankind that nature was the dominant earthly force, an act designed to puncture human hubris.

The English writer Thomas Hardy was one of the earliest to write about the loss of the *Titanic*. In 'The Convergence of the Twain' (1912), he wrote:

Photograph of Robert Falcon Scott and party at the South Pole, 17 January 1912 (taken by using a string to pull the shutter of the camera).

Prepared a sinister mate
For her – so gaily great –
A Shape of Ice, for the time far and dissociate.

And as the smart ship grew smart
In stature, grace, and hue
In shadowy silent distance grew the Iceberg too.

Alien they seemed to be:
No mortal eye could see
The intimate welding of their later history.[27]

Written for the Titanic Disaster Fund, Hardy's poem is unusual and uses the term 'sinister mate' to describe the iceberg that decided the fate of the ship. The 'intimate welding' is clearly an unwelcome one as steel and ice come into contact with one another. The end result was a disastrous conflagration between human, ship and sea ice.

What made the sinking all the more significant was timing, coming just days after the demise of Scott and his Antarctic party in late March 1912 (but not revealed to the wider world until February 1913). We might even identify 1912 as a high-water mark in global public engagement with ice. A Norwegian party led by Roald Amundsen had finally reached the elusive South Pole and a British-built liner once thought of as unsink-able had been lost in the icy-filled seas off Newfoundland. As with the loss of the Scott party, there were tales of heroism and self-sacrifice mingled with accusations of incompetence and mishap. What is striking is that there has never been another sinking of the magnitude of the RMS *Titanic* as a result of ice. The latest disaster involving an iceberg, in 2007, resulted in the loss of MV *Explorer* in Antarctica, but all on board were rescued.

From being terrified of ice to terrifying the ice

While the aesthetic legacy of the sublime and its relationship to ice in Western cultures endures, the sublime itself has mutated. Compared to the nineteenth century, when awe, fascination and terror dominated literary and visual representations, our rela-tionship with ice has shifted from a technological sublime where we have celebrated our capacity to master it to a post-human sublime where ice loss is used to speculate on the future of humanity itself. Aesthetically, our mountains, poles, oceans and glaciers have been 'harvested' by explorers, artists, scientists and novelists more than ever before. On a daily basis, we can access articles, books and news media warning of loss, instability and shrinkage. The monstrous icebergs that confronted the *Titanic* in the North Atlantic seem far removed from more contem-porary accounts of the thinning and retreat of sea ice. We may still be 'moved' by ice but have our cultural and imaginative registers shifted?

This shift is not straightforward, however. There are plenty of accounts of terrifying ice and awe-inspiring ice by modern-day mountaineers and explorers. Adventure documentary films such as *Touching the Void* (2003, based in part on the autobiography of Joe Simpson's climbing experiences) and *The Summit* (2012) continue to trade in a sublime aesthetic which posits ice as raw, overwhelming and mysterious – an environment where humans have sometimes to make desperate choices in order to survive.[28] Here the mountain, as a material and lively object, is posited as capacious and capricious, capable of unleashing immense forces that cause avalanches and snow blizzards – and yet also capable of revealing and exposing a complex underground space, beneath glaciers and moraines, capable of saving and entombing the fortunate and unfortunate respectively. For Joe Simpson, who was thrown down a deep ice crevasse while climbing, the labyrinth of subterranean ice actually gave him a way out. He managed, counter-intuitively, to descend further into the crevasse where he found a hole to climb back on to the glacier and eventually after days of crawling with a broken leg and close to starvation made it back to base camp. He was very lucky. Sadly, the bodies of the dead simply stay where they died. In one infamous example, the 'Green Boots' body of Tsewang Paljor remained where he died in 1996 for over fifteen years before it was finally removed for burial.

While the ice can seem infinite and never-ending in the mountain-climbing and polar accounts of some, it is also provisional and vulnerable to others. In *Chasing Ice* (2012), *National Geographic* photographer and writer James Balog addresses his initial scepticism about climate change and claims relating to ice loss due to anthropogenic warming. Using time-lapse video, he develops a visual narrative encompassing multi-year records of glaciers and their well-being. In his rendition, the horror of ice loss forces him and viewers to confront the unthinkable – a world without ice. He is, by the end of his personal odyssey, a convert to the existence of anthropogenic climate change.[29]

The natural world becomes both an object of terror and, as it melts, an existential threat to human continuity. The viewer is asked to ponder what happens when the ice goes or stops being able to reveal secrets about our past and possible future – will we continue to tell such stories with ice and invest in ice a tremendous capacity to be characterful (such as friendly, hostile, horrible, beautiful), dynamic (freezing, melting and in motion) and embodied (felt, experienced, and the stuff of dreams and nightmares)? Or will we have to find other substances to do such imaginative labour?

What is left unsaid, however, is whether these experiential reflections of ice loss are in any shape or form sufficient to disrupt global capitalism and fossil-fuel-based economies. Recalling Bruce Robbins's accounting of the 'sweatshop sublime', there may be fleeting moments when we realize our own position (and indeed benefits we might accrue) in some vast totality such as global capitalism. However, those epiphanies often fail to move us to action because we struggle to

The body of 'Green Boots' climber (later identified as Tsewang Paljor), who was part of the ill-fated Indo-Tibetan Border Police Expedition.

connect the everyday lives of ourselves to those of indigenous peoples in Greenland through myriad networks, relationships and objects.[30] We retreat into an 'everyday smallness' in order to escape the scale and extent of the totality. From indigenous Arctic film-makers to Western novelists, there is arguably a renaissance of interest with the sublime, emphasizing new and disturbing inhuman ecologies.

Ice's position within our ecological and cultural division of labour inspires, sustains, entertains and preserves us. If we continue to abuse it, unnatural and monstrous consequences will surely follow.

4 Icy Geopolitics

The icy reaches of the Earth have not escaped the grasp of geo-political actors and interests. But it took time and spatial circum-stances to prompt it. The British geographer and member of parliament Halford Mackinder (1861–1947) was interested in the role of what he called 'heartland' powers such as Russia and Germany. For Mackinder, who had travelled to Africa and Asia, the Arctic Ocean was the peripheral extreme of a continental mass thought to be pivotal to global geopolitical history. In his famous 1904 paper, 'The Geographical Pivot of History', the accompanying maps of what he termed the 'heartland' depict the Arctic Ocean as simply 'icy sea', indicative of relative immobility and blockage. Future great powers would be drawn, in his judge-ment, to the southern Euro-Asian landmass because of its popu-lation, resources and transport linkages to the wider world.[1] He could not imagine the Arctic ever being more than an 'icy sea'.

The Canadian writer and explorer Vilhjalmur Stefansson (1879–1962) took a different view. Of Icelandic heritage, he studied at Harvard and travelled to Iceland and later Alaska and the Canadian Arctic where he conducted exploratory and ethnographic work with indigenous communities. His reputa-tion as a polar explorer is mixed, built on a catalogue of failures and misjudgements, but is also one based on living with indigen-ous communities and learning about their language and cultures. He became more widely known after the publication of *The Friendly Arctic* (1921), which posited the idea that the Arctic region was hospitable and filled with resources. Stefansson's goal was to educate the North American public about the Arctic and challenge head-on the notion that the northern latitudes should be represented as a proverbial wasteland and altogether peripheral region. But he also attracted opprobrium from his fellow explorers, including the famous Norwegian Roald Amundsen, who branded the Canadian a mendacious charlatan who refused to recognize that the Arctic was a dangerous and far from 'friendly' place for those seeking to settle and exploit it on the scale envisaged. Amundsen was, of course, to be claimed by the Arctic via a plane crash in 1928 while seeking the whereabouts of his friend and fellow explorer, Umberto Nobile. Sean Connery, the original James Bond, played Amundsen in a Soviet-Italian film (*The Red Tent*, 1969) about the quest to find Nobile in the Arctic Ocean.

Stefansson contributed to the articulation of a popular geopolitics of the Arctic through his skilful if controversial advocacy for a 'friendly Arctic'. He drew attention to the Arctic's peoples and resources but also urged readers and listeners to look to their maps. He reminded his audiences that the ancient Greeks had taken a far more positive view of the north, a Hyperborea, imagining it to be more akin to a paradise than wasteland. Difficult to enter, but for those who made it there awaited a veritable feast for the eyes and body – a world filled with a fecund

Stefansson

STEFANSSON AND HIS PARTY LEAVING THE *KARLUK*

Vilhjalmur Stefansson and his Canadian Arctic Expedition party leaving the whaling ship *Karluk*, 20 September 1913.

Roald Amundsen and Umberto Nobile's airship *Norge* at Ny-Alesund, Svalbard, 7 May 1926.

ecosystem, where the passing seasons were immaterial. Writing in *National Geographic* magazine in 1922, Stefansson pressed home this view of the Arctic:

> The map of the Northern Hemisphere shows that the Arctic Ocean is a huge Mediterranean. It lies between the continents somewhat as the Mediterranean lies between Europe and Africa. In the past it has been an impassable Mediterranean. In the near future, it will not only become passable, but will become a favourite air route between the continents, at least at certain seasons – safer, more comfortable, and consisting of shorter 'hops' than any other air route that lies across the oceans that separate the present-day centres of population.[2]

In the final decade and a half of his life, Stefansson witnessed what was possible if money and imagination were invested in the Arctic region. The Second World War demonstrated that the Arctic and Antarctic were of interest to both Axis and Allied Powers. German submarines transformed the North Atlantic and parts of the Arctic Ocean into a dangerous environment for the Allied convoys supporting the Soviet Union. War planners were desperate for greater understanding of polar weather and sea ice, and its capacity to interfere or even facilitate the conduct of warfare (for example, hide and obscure enemy ships and planes). Stefansson never envisaged war in his 'friendly Arctic' but the onset of the Second World War did transform the maritime and coastal Arctic into a war zone. Charting one's way through ice, snow and inclement seas was the new priority, not economic development of the sort he imagined. But what he had recognized, albeit with war rather than resource development as the primary driver, was the manner in which the northern dimension of global geopolitics was being recalibrated. By the 1950s, nuclear-powered submarines and ice-breaker capacity clearly offered up

uss *Skate* at the North Pole, 1959.

new possibilities for breaking through and transiting under prevailing sea ice. Ice disrupted sonar and provided places to hide. Its slippery nature served slippery geopolitical ends. Passageways such as the Northwest Passage and Northern Sea Route (directly off the northern Russian/Soviet coastline) assumed ever-greater importance from the mid-twentieth century onwards, and opened up the Arctic Ocean region more generally to far greater potential for movement of military and civilian shipping that was both destination-orientated as well as transitional.

The Cold War encouraged an array of what we might term 'icy geopolitics', routed through and under the ice, but also rooted on the ice. Facilitating cartographic and physical possession required investment in maps, flags, bases and extensive travel over and on mountains, ice sheets, sea ice and ice caps. Mapping and surveying were an essential prelude to the claiming of formal sovereignty, and in the ice-filled regions of the world 'effective occupation' brought its own particular challenges for human occupiers and their equipment. Ice-filled regions are rarely free from contention either, as their borders become enrolled in dispute and contestation. In the mountain and glacial regions of South Asia, India, Pakistan and China have faced off with one another for decades, marshalling their armed forces some 6,000 m (20,000 ft) above sea level, with dire consequences for human welfare. Occupying the high point, and claims to physical mastery of space and the body, have been emblematic of nationalistic discourses and resistance to invading forces.

In these iterations of icy geopolitics, ice and the extremes of weather that often characterize such environments both facilitate and impede colonial and national projects.[3] Empty ice can and does appear inviting but that same ice can also be challenging and recalcitrant in exposing attempts to colonize, settle and administer. Naming helped in part to bind a mobile and recalcitrant material but it can still play mischief with international borders, inspiring the formal recognition in Italy of the 'movable border': when glaciers retreat they alter the placement of border markers and assessment of boundaries based on watershed dynamics. In the Arctic, Antarctic and mountainous regions of the world, there is no shortage of reminders of how the ice could impede travel, destroy infrastructure and exercise a ruinous influence on the unlucky souls stationed on often remote outposts. Unlike in temperate and tropical regions of the world, population density tends to be low, and traditional markers of colonization and settlement such as fields, hedges and roads harder to establish and build, let alone maintain. The movement of ice, in combination with unforgiving darkness and cold, could also initiate havoc on geopolitical scheming. Expeditions have got lost, planes have crashed, ships have become trapped and bases have been crushed by the ebb and flow of ice sheets. But as our auditing of icy geopolitics should recognize, the world's icy regions have also inspired forms of co-operation and diplomacy that are the envy of the world. Science diplomacy has arguably seen one of its most powerful manifestations in the creation and maintenance of the Antarctic as the world's first zone of peace.

Owning ice

When we examine a political map of our Earth, the eye is drawn to the mosaic of pictures and lines that represent around two hundred nation-states and their respective national territories. When accounting for land ownership, there are few parts of the Earth that have not been claimed either by individuals or by some sort of political entity, whether it be a local council, canton, regional organization, national body or global authority. If you look closely, the most striking exception to this simple rule is Antarctica and if you look in even finer detail, it is possible to detect a series of uncertainties and disputes over international boundaries, some of which involve remote regions of the world covered by ice and snow. The foundations on which our international political system rests owe much of their origin to modern European states and their mainly temperate and low-lying regions.

Glaciers, ice sheets and ice caps continue to prove challenging to modern sovereignty. The political history of Antarctica has fundamentally been shaped by events over the last two hundred

The Hindu-Kush
mountain range in
Afghanistan, with the
remnants of a Soviet
T-62 tank in the
foreground.

years. Nineteenth-century exploration and exploitation began to
reveal a continent shrouded with ice and fog and surrounded by
water. Early twentieth-century maps were sketchy, acknowledg-
ing a body of ice and rock but uncertainty was rife as to whether
it was composed of at least two ice masses. European and North
American geographers and explorers were eager to 'fill in the
gaps', and governments led by the UK initiated a 'scramble for
Antarctica' in 1908 when they registered the first territorial claim
to the icy continent. Just as the embers inflaming the 'scramble
for Africa' were fading in the 1890s, so a new scramble started
further south.

Ice was treated as frozen ground and thus considered capable
of being claimed and administered. In the absence of a native
indigenous population, and having not been claimed by other
parties beforehand, the Antarctic was classified as *terra nullius* – land belonging to no one. As the 1885 Berlin Conference
regarding Africa had already determined, any territory regarded
as *terra nullius* required interested parties to show evidence of
effective occupation of the claimed land. Once authority was
established, through markers of ownership, then the occupying
party notified others that the territory in question was no longer
to be considered *terra nullius*. Building bases and establishing
post offices followed.

With the help of two dominion partners, Australia and New Zealand, the British-Imperial partnership began to extend those claims over Antarctica and charge others, such as Norway, taxes for exploiting and processing whales at their whaling stations on islands such as South Georgia (whale oil and bone were lucrative commodities).[4] Twentieth-century authorities such as the British MP and Conservative secretary for state Leopold Amery envisaged Antarctica as an extension of the imperial project. Between 1919 and 1928, this was official British policy – to envisage the polar continent as an exclusively British possession. This plan became unstuck when France and later Norway pressed their own claims to Antarctica. They also had a history of exploration, effective occupation and notification to draw upon and did so in 1923 and 1939 respectively. On the eve of the Second World War, Argentina and Chile followed suit but critically did not believe that they were mimicking European claimants; rather, they were merely exercising inherited rights from a fifteenth-century papal decree, which divided the world for the basis of global exploration between Spain and Portugal. As successor states to the Spanish Empire in the Americas, Argentina and Chile believed that the Antarctic realm closest to South America

The British Antarctic Base A (Port Lockroy) on the Antarctic Peninsula, now a major tourist attraction.

Flensing a whale (removing the blubber) at the whaling factory in Grytviken, South Georgia, March 1916.

was a natural extension of their territories. They joined the UK, Australia, New Zealand, France and Norway as claimant states.

Claiming, exploiting and settling Antarctica offered something quite enticing. It looked and felt like 'empty land'. Unlike other places declared *terra nullius,* such as Australia, there was no indigenous human population. The ice appeared to support either inedible penguins or edible and commercially valuable seals and whales. Fishing was to come much later. With 99 per cent of Antarctica covered by ice, everything had to be imported from elsewhere. Building bases and evidencing 'effective occupation' required constructive and political labour. Looking busy was an imperative. In the Antarctic Peninsula, Argentina, Chile and the United Kingdom all believed that they owned the same territory, and they sent men to map, survey and evaluate the area in question. Post offices were established so that letters could be stamped with British, Argentine and Chilean postage stamps. A 'paper war' erupted. By 1950 seven claims were made and two countries (the United States and the Soviet Union) reserved their own rights to make claims in the future. Only one portion of Antarctica remained unclaimed because it was so remote from existing activities; to this day it remains a terrestrial oddity. Everywhere else is claimed by one state or another.

Soviet postage stamp of the International Geophysical Year, 1959.

What brought international agreement to this disputed territory was the International Geophysical Year (IGY, 1957–8), coupled with a realization that the interested parties were not able to settle their differences armed with nineteenth-century notions of *terra nullius* and 'effective occupation'.[5] The world had changed radically since the Treaty of Berlin in 1885. Icy Antarctica might have been unoccupied but the mood music regarding European colonialism altered when the United States and the Soviet Union assumed the role of superpowers. Both were avowedly anti-colonial and both participated in the IGY, a period of eighteen months devoted to global scientific study, with the goal of demonstrating that Antarctica was an international area without meaningful national boundaries. In the name of science and common humanity, they swept away those de facto international divisions. It was a compelling move as the ice was internationalized rather than nationalized. Both superpowers established a string of IGY bases and notably selected the heart of the continent (the U.S. at South Pole Station) and the remotest and coldest point, namely the Pole of Relative Inaccessibility (the Soviet Union), to showcase their infrastructural and geopolitical power.

Within a year of the IGY ending, the United States convened a conference to discuss the future of Antarctica. The twelve IGY Antarctic countries, including the seven claimants and other IGY parties such as Belgium, Japan and South Africa, agreed on an Antarctic Treaty, which declared that the continent should be devoted to peace and science. Uniquely, it declared the continent to be a demilitarized, nuclear-free zone, quite an achievement in the midst of the Cold War. The parties agreed that the disputed sovereignty of Antarctica should be put to one side in order to secure co-operation. Ownership was not settled; rather it was deferred. Antarctica received further protection in the form of the 1991 Protocol on Environmental Protection, which entered into force in 1998.

Owning glaciers

On a smaller scale, heavily glaciated countries such as Switzerland have developed their own arrangements regarding the ownership and management of glaciers. In the Swiss Civil Code, glaciers are distinguished under Article 664 as public water bodies similar to lakes and rivers.[6] As objects of law, the glacier is assumed to be unsuitable for cultivation (and thus legally and geographically distinct from pasture which can be owned and cultivated) and classified as public property for common usage. But the exact legal regime beyond that governing glaciated environments varies from canton to canton, and access and usage is regulated accordingly. The only hotel ever established was on the Rhône glacier, the Hôtel Glacier du Rhône, and was occupied in effect by a pioneering tourist family called Seiler. The hotel remains to this day but it is no longer possible under Swiss law to acquire property rights on glaciers.

The intersection between ice and pasture can create its own local political tension in countries like Switzerland. Where does pasture begin and end? What happens if ice retreats and pasture expands due to soil being exposed and cultivated by grasses? Are boundaries able to move legally? As with international borders, the edge of ice, mountain peaks and cardinal points played their part in helping to discern these glacial-pastoral environments as a series of legal-geographical landscapes. Descriptions of borders and regions, articulated centuries ago, often fail to match contemporary observation. Before the nineteenth century, the fate of glaciated regions was largely determined by imaginative rather

than legal intervention. Glaciers were objects to be marvelled at, clambered over and ultimately feared. As national law expanded its remit, the federal state and the cantons assumed further control over what could be done with glaciers.

Hôtel Glacier du Rhône, Switzerland.

In the last fifty years, glaciers have become part and parcel of everyday legal regimes. As their value has been recognized – environmentally, aesthetically and commercially – the application of law has increased. The regulation of skiing areas provides one obvious example of where local authorities are eager to exert control over what can be done, what can be built and who profits from winter skiers and summer walkers. Objects and infrastructure need maintenance and regulation – cable cars, walking trails, ski runs, roads and the like. Accidents and disasters impose burdens on authorities and insurance companies, and health and safety regulations regarding access to glaciers are not inconsiderable. Sometimes the physical forces of glacial action can simply overwhelm any safety considerations. In August 1965, the tongue of the Allalin glacier in the Swiss Alps broke away and killed 88 workers constructing a dam in the vicinity. The ownership of ice brings with it a litany of challenges, from the diplomatic to the compensatory.

As an energy resource, glaciers also attract legal and regulatory attention. Many countries including Norway and Switzerland, and mountain chains such as the Himalayas, have attracted critical infrastructure projects, including dams and hydroelectric plants. Glaciers are major water resources and provide essential water supply to river systems such as the Indus and Ganges in South Asia. The construction, ownership and protection of dams are deemed vital to individual countries and their sense of national security. Glaciers can attract both environmental and military protection. In Switzerland, federal and canton authorities have to collaborate with one another in order to fulfil distinct functions, including protecting glaciers designated as UNESCO World

The Norwegian Glacier Museum in Fjaerland, Norway.

Heritage Sites and managing and regulating the thirteen glacier ski regions. Cable car development is often one of the more controversial elements in decision making because of its aesthetic impact, but also what greater accessibility to high Alpine regions brings in terms of economic development, environmental impact and legal responsibilities.

In 1991 European countries such as Switzerland, Austria, Italy and Germany agreed upon an Alpine Convention, addressing the protection of the Alps. While recognizing national sovereignty over parts of the glaciers and ice sheets of the mountain range, it also noted that international co-operation was required for effective monitoring and protection. Covering some 190,000 square km (75,000 square mi.), with 14 million residents in the vicinity and nearly 6,000 municipalities involved in some form of local administration, the challenges are considerable in the face of ongoing climate change and resource and economic development pressures. Every year the parties meet to discuss an array of issues including natural hazards, water resources, pasture management, ecology, human usage, transport and tourism.

Strangely, the Convention makes no explicit mention of ice, snow or permafrost. But the Preamble recognized that the parties were:

> AWARE that the Alps are one of the largest continuous unspoilt natural areas in Europe, which, with their outstanding unique and diverse natural habitat, culture and history, constitute an economic, cultural, recreational and living environment in the heart of Europe, shared by numerous peoples and countries.

Had it been negotiated twenty years later, the Alpine Convention might have foregrounded the very thing that makes the Alps distinctive: namely snow and ice. The Convention, however, is clear on one thing: it acknowledges the national sovereignty of the eight parties over their respective elements of the snow- and ice-covered areas of the Alps. But the extractive potential is shrinking and all parties might ask themselves about whether a 'tipping point' is fast approaching where these areas cannot be harvested in the same way.[7]

Immovable borders

International borders matter to states. They represent the limits of jurisdiction and demarcate claims to ownership including the use of resources. Glacial environments may often be remote and poorly connected to national infrastructure but they do add resource, environmental, aesthetic and cultural value to local and national communities. Vague treaties between states and poorly drawn maps of borderlands can and do cause conflict, and any form of geopolitical division is made more complicated when the environment in question is remote, unstable or confusing to those attempting to delimit a boundary and demarcate through a treaty. International boundaries drawn on a map do not specify a particular width, and it might not be clear what was being imagined – a ditch, a fence, a ridge, a river, and/or a line of trees. Boundary markers, especially in remote areas, can also simply disappear because of avalanches, landslides or deliberate obfuscation by parties in dispute with one another.

In the glaciated areas of the world, the challenges are considerable and perhaps none more so than the infamous standoff between India and Pakistan over the high-altitude glacial area called Siachen. It is officially the highest battlefield in the world and extreme weather and hostile terrain extract a terrible price on those who serve there. The genesis of this extraordinary conflict lies in the 1947–8 Indo-Pakistani conflict and the subsequent 1949 Karachi Agreement, which addressed the highly disputed area of Kashmir. The Ceasefire Line was established by reference to map co-ordinate NJ9842 but thereafter it was simply described as extending 'north to the glaciers'. The presumption in 1949 was that nobody would be terribly concerned about glacial wastelands – thinly populated as they were and deemed of little resource value. The area in question was the Siachen Glacier, 75 km (46 mi.) long, located east of the Karakoram Range of the Himalayas. The 1972 Simla Agreement, after another round of

A French border marker between France and Italy, which is only visible in the summer months.

conflict between the two countries, transformed the Ceasefire Line into a Line of Control but failed to address ambiguities in the northern extremes of the Indo-Pakistani border.

In the late 1970s, ambivalence about Siachen Glacier changed when Indian authorities discovered something surprising. American maps appeared to extend the Line of Control northwards in a manner that ensured that the territory appeared under Pakistani control. India was also alarmed that its rival was licensing mountaineers to climb mountains in the disputed area without informing New Delhi. Worried about future Pakistani intentions, India dispatched soldiers to the area in April 1984 and established de facto control over the main glacier and tributary glaciers and strategic passes. Both sides, since the mid-1980s, have exchanged gunfire and threatened one another with armed assault. Since 2003 a ceasefire has been established and largely respected around what is termed the Actual Ground Position Line (AGPL).

The greatest enemy to confront both sides is physical. Operating at heights of 7,000–8,000 m (23,000–26,000 ft), the temperatures descend to minus 40°C (minus 40°F) and winds exceed 300 km (186 mi.) per hour. Oxygen levels are low and soldiers frequently complain that they endure hallucination, damage to

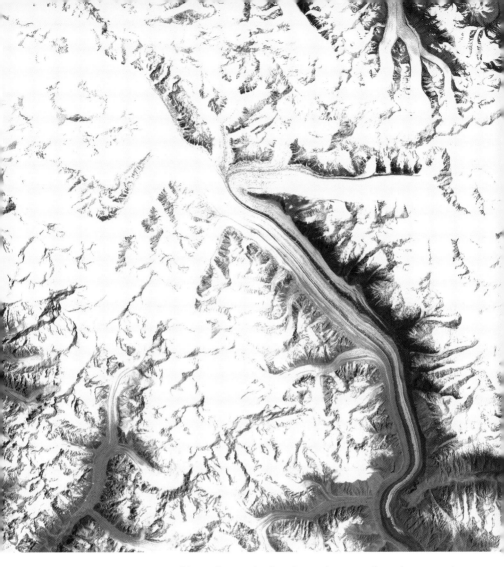

NASA image of the
Siachen Glacier.

memory, blurred speech, frostbite, sleeping disorders, weight
loss, pulmonary oedema and mental health deterioration. While
soldiers do receive specialist training, the restrictions and con-
strictions are formidable with limits to operating areas, near
constant dangers of avalanches and crevasses, restricted availability of fresh food and limited medical facilities. Helicopters
operating in the region are often grounded because of severe
weather. Since the 1980s, around 2,000 soldiers on both sides
have lost their lives or been left with long-term or permanent

medical problems. In February 2016 an avalanche claimed the lives of ten Indian soldiers, including one who was thought to have survived six days buried in 11 m (35 ft) of snow. It followed on from a similar disaster in 2012, which engulfed a Pakistani base and took more than 120 lives. Any resolution to the crisis will depend on the two countries finding agreement about how and where the Line of Control might actually extend northwards.

Movable borders

In many parts of the world, international borders have followed rivers, mountains and other geographical features such as deserts and floodplains. Termed 'natural borders', the use of physical geographical features to demarcate is rooted in human history, including the ancient Greek and Roman empires, which in order to expand and colonize had to traverse mountains, seas and rivers. Defining the edge of the nation, however, was not straight-forward. Natural borders may not be stable. Rivers can and do shift their course. Mountains and in particular glaciers and snow-fields melt, change shape and even retreat. In the Alps, where ice and snow loss has been profound, Switzerland, Italy and France have had to negotiate over their shifting borders, most of which were settled in the nineteenth century but some were not settled finally until the Second World War. In the Alps, rivers and glaciers were essential to border delimitation. The high points of glaciers were commonly chosen to identify points from which lines could be constructed as part of that border work. Climate change has contributed to overall warming and a shift in the glacial geographies of the Alps, with the net effect being that the high point and crests of glaciers and watersheds are in flux. It is feared that glaciers could disappear by 2050 in many parts of the Alps if the warming trend continues.

Italy and Switzerland share a border of some 750 km (465 mi.) and in some places, like the Basodino Glacier, the border has shifted by metres, which may not sound significant given the remoteness and inaccessibility of the region but is some-thing that can become the object of nationalist discord in other parts of the world. Bilateral agreements have been entered into and aerial photography and photogrammetry have been used to redefine those borders. In May 2009 the Italian government at the time introduced new legislation formally identifying the border as movable and thus not fixed. The relevant piece of legislation was entitled 'Ratification and Implementation of the Exchange of Notes between the Italian Republic and the Swiss Confederation concerning the "Mobile" Borders on the Ridge or Watershed Line, made in Rome on 23 and 26 May 2008'.[8]

Any alteration to a national border, even when located in un-inhabited and remote areas such as a mountaintop or an ice sheet, carries with it the possibility of nationalist sentiment animated by suspicion. In Argentina and Chile, the mapping and surveying of the countries are largely in the hands of military geographers and what used to be called Military Geography Institutes (now the National Geographic Institute in Argentina). Separated by the Andes, the two countries share a long border stretching some 5,600 km (3,500 mi.) from desert landscapes in the north to ice sheets and sheer mountains in southern Patagonia and beyond to the Beagle Channel and Drake's Passage. Both countries make claims to the Antarctic Peninsula region. The legal groundwork for the delimitation of their common border began in 1881 and remains a work in progress as the remote, high-altitude and ice-filled portions of their southern borderlands have proven difficult and highly sensitive to political and public opinion.

Dominated by military regimes in the 1970s and '80s, border delimitation was caught up in a wider geopolitical intrigue that made co-operation difficult. The presence of the United Kingdom in the South Atlantic complicated things still further for Argentina in particular. Despite improvements in the post-democratic era in the late 1980s, a dispute over the Laguna del Desierto (Lake of the Desert) in the early 1990s served as a reminder that remote and uninhabited places can inflame political passions. Located in the northern fringe of the Southern Patagonian Ice Field, it is more accessible to Argentina than Chile because of the relative position of the valleys, glaciers and rivers. The dispute went to international arbitration and the boundary was moved so that Argentina's claims were prioritized over Chile's. The decision was finally accepted by Chile, after an appeal in 1995, but the more southerly areas of the borderlands remained disputed.[9]

In 2008 both countries reached agreement over the last section of the border in the Southern Patagonian Ice Field, which is heavily glaciated and provides vital water supplies in the spring and summer for southern communities. That final 50-km (30-mi.) section still requires bilateral agreement and parliamentary approval for the border to be established, with agreement that glacial melting in the future might once again force the border to potentially move. If all else fails then maybe the two countries might take inspiration from a Norwegian initiative to

Aerial photograph of the Southern Patagonian Ice Field.

shift the international boundary with Finland in order to 'gift' a mountain to the latter on the eve of their hundredth-anniversary independence celebrations in 2017.

Movable ice

Sea ice is in legal terms rather different to ice that is situated on or attached to land. It moves, it can be towed (provoking interesting questions about ownership) and is sometimes deliberately broken up. If part of the marine environment, then ice comes under the provisions of the United Nations Law of the Sea Convention (UNCLOS). Apart from one specific article, Article 234 on 'ice-covered waters', the world's seas and oceans are assumed to be in the main free from ice. But Article 234 matters greatly to Arctic states such as Canada and Russia because as the nearest coastal states they are granted special powers:

> Coastal States have the right to adopt and enforce non-discriminatory laws and regulations for the prevention, reduction and control of marine pollution from vessels in ice-covered areas within the limits of the exclusive economic zone, where particularly severe climatic conditions and the presence of ice covering such areas for most of the year create obstructions or exceptional hazards to navigation, and pollution of the marine environment could cause major harm to or irreversible disturbance of the ecological balance. Such laws and regulations shall have due regard to navigation and the protection and preservation of the marine environment based on the best available scientific evidence.[10]

There are many areas of the marine world where sea ice is either constant or a seasonal phenomenon and, as in Article 234 where there is ice for 'most of the year' (that is, a minimum of six months and one day), then coastal states can impose special environmental regulations on users. Sea ice is a major challenge for busy shipping areas such as the Baltic and parts of the eastern seaboard of Canada and the northern United States, as well as around the Russian Far East including the Sea of Japan. The Great Lakes experience substantial lake ice each winter, requiring ice-breaker engagement and the involvement of the U.S. and Canadian Coast Guards. In the Arctic region, one of the Earth's fabled sea routes is the Northwest Passage (NWP), which countless European explorers and their sponsors believed held the key to a new world filled with trading and commercial opportunities. Sea ice and inclement weather posed a major obstacle to those adventurers and sailors, and even now there is only modest search and rescue capacity in many parts of the region. It remains a challenging and difficult place to navigate.

For Canada, the legal status of the NWP has been a long-standing preoccupation with successive governments contending that the passageway is part of the country's 'historic waters' rather than an acknowledged international transit route.[11] The United States believes that the NWP fulfils the legal criteria for a maritime passage connecting the high seas of the Atlantic and Arctic Oceans. The distinction is not mere wordplay because national and international rights depend upon the designation

MS *Viking* at Helsinki Port, Finland.

U.S. Coast Guard vessel the *Polar Star*, which made a controversial voyage (without the authorization of the Canadian government) in 1985 through the Northwest Passage.

of the NWP. If 'historic waters', the passageway would be a body of water where the coastal state (in this case Canada) could impose greater restrictions on others trying to pass through it. In contrast, an international transit passage under international maritime law is something that third parties can travel through with fewer constraints. Canada argues that the NWP has never been a route for international transit because of prevailing sea ice, low levels of international shipping demand and its geographical length and complexity. It remains comparatively poorly mapped and charted.

The control and regulation of the NWP pivot around both historic usage and the hazard imposed by sea ice. The two intersected most notably in the late 1960s when an American-owned tanker, SS *Manhattan*, made the first commercial voyage of the NWP as part of an initial operation to see whether North Slope/Alaskan oil could be transported to the 'Lower 48', let alone European markets, via the Canadian Arctic. Pipeline construction would be expensive and involve lengthy negotiations with indigenous peoples. Shipping Alaskan oil looked attractive

Oil waste from the grounding of the *Exxon Valdez* in March 1989 off Prince William Sound, Alaska, United States.

because there was only one stakeholder to deal with – the Canadian government. The voyage alarmed the Canadian government. Prime Minister Pierre Trudeau feared that if the ss *Manhattan* completed the transit voyage this would set a precedent for future commercial traffic. It did but it required considerable Canadian ice-breaker assistance. While there was Canadian sensitivity to u.s. operations in the North American Arctic, economics (the opening of the Trans-Alaska Pipeline) rather than geopolitics resolved the issue.

Scarred by the ss *Manhattan* voyage, the Canadian government invoked environmental stewardship as a counter-measure. Invoking the spectre of disaster, sea ice was positioned as a hazard to 'safe shipping' and one that required the Canadian authorities to regulate further. No one, after all, could possibly wish to see the 1967 ss *Torrey Canyon* disaster (which spilled oil off the Cornish coastline) reproduced in the Arctic. Under the terms of the 1970 Arctic Waters Pollution Prevention Act (AWPPA), further safety obligations were placed on those who wished to travel through Canadian Arctic waters. Canada also began to promote its ice agenda at the ongoing international negotiations over UNCLOS. With the support of Russia, Article 234 of UNCLOS helped to allay Canadian concerns over the NWP. It allowed coastal states to protect ice-covered waters against marine pollution from commercial vessels operating within 200 nautical miles of their coastline.

Sea ice is viewed as a major shipping hazard. Prime Minister Pierre Trudeau warned audiences in 1970 that super-tankers 'make ludicrous the word "spill"', and that international maritime law had not addressed the emerging environmental threat posed by oil and other pollutants being spilled into marine and ice-covered environments. The movement of oil tankers through fragile Arctic waters demanded urgent action and Canada was positioning itself as a special guardian of North American waters and sea ice. Article 234 of UNCLOS is often cited by Canadian authorities as one of the greatest triumphs of national diplomacy. Ice-covered waters were recognized as deserving special protection, and proximate coastal states should be allowed to impose higher environmental standards on those seeking to transit polar waters. Disasters, however, have occurred in northern waters. In March 1989 the *Exxon Valdez* ran aground on a reef in Prince William Sound, Alaska. The accident was caused because the ship's captain was trying to avoid icebergs in the relatively narrow shipping lane. Some 11 million U.S. gallons of oil was lost, affecting over 1,000 miles of Alaskan coastline, killing hundreds of thousands of seabirds and other species. In 2004 a federal judge ordered Exxon to pay $4.5 billion in punitive damages. The company was criticized for its poor response to the disaster and the incident has long served as a warning of the inherent dangers of operating large vessels in ice-covered waters.

While Canadian commentators continue to encourage the United States to recognize the NWP as 'historic waters' of Canada, there is little evidence that the position of their southern neighbour will change. Diminishing sea ice in the Arctic Ocean might also weaken the claim that northern waters are quite as ice-covered as they once were, especially in the summer season. Arctic tourism might also be a key driver in the future with regard to shipping traffic while the implementation of the International Maritime Organization's Polar Code in January 2017 should improve safety standards and possibly serve as reminder about how Canadian leadership on Arctic marine stewardship was a product of a particular moment in environmental disaster and geopolitical history. Would Canada have succeeded in promoting Article 234 to UNCLOS a few decades later when the fate of Arctic sea ice was conceptualized in very different ways – as something that was disappearing and more vulnerable to ongoing ocean warming and no longer present for 'most of the year'?[12]

Alternatives to icy geopolitics

Thus far our reflection on icy geopolitics has been overwhelmingly influenced by a consideration of states and their involvement in international regimes and organizations. Sometimes ice has acted as an opportunity to disrupt dominant geopolitical logics of enclosure and bordering. In 2004 a joint Israeli-Palestinian expedition climbed a 2,700-m (9,000-ft) mountain near Bruce Plateau (named after the Scottish naturalist William Speirs Bruce, 1867–1921) in Antarctica. At the summit, they formally named the peak The Mountain of Israeli-Palestinian Friendship and declared:

> We, the members of Breaking the Ice, the Israeli-Palestinian expedition to Antarctica, having reached the conclusion of a long journey by land and sea from our homes in the Middle East to the southernmost reaches of the Earth, now stand atop this unnamed mountain. By reaching its summit we have proven that Palestinians and Israelis can cooperate with one another with mutual respect and trust.[13]

In the Arctic region, indigenous peoples have had a very particular relationship to sea and land ice which is quite different from dominant geopolitical optics. Rather than being a resource to be controlled and surveyed, ice enables mobility and access to essential food sources such as fish, marine birds, seals and whales. Indigenous peoples in the Arctic pre-dated the modern nation-state system by some millennia. For a predominantly oral culture, Inuit and indigenous traditional knowledge in general was communicated through storytelling, not

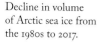

Decline in volume of Arctic sea ice from the 1980s to 2017.

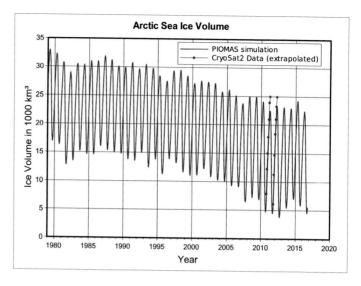

via map-making in a Western sense. For those who lived in the region, the Arctic was and is an environment composed of a network of trails linking circumpolar communities to fishing lakes, hunting grounds and other food supplies needed to ensure survival from one season to another. Place names and trails are integral to Inuit heritage and specify their long-standing relationships to ice, land and water. Names also described ice formations and pathways across the ice. Produced by colleagues at Canadian and UK universities, the Pan-Inuit Trails project used a series of interactive maps to show how indigenous mapping of the Canadian Arctic did not coincide at all with the provincial and territorial boundaries of the modern Canadian nation-state.[14]

The initiative was timely, alongside other projects such as the Atlas of Inuit Sea Ice Knowledge and Use based on the experiences and memories of indigenous communities around Cape Dorset in the Canadian Arctic.[15] Inuit movement and occupation of the ice is directly connected to indigenous geopolitics, especially at a moment when there is unprecedented interest in the resources and sovereignty of the Arctic region. Inuit trails and tracks are not marked in the same way as roads, railways and airports. They are not permanent or semi-permanent features akin to modern infrastructure; rather, the routes are often seasonal, subtle to outsiders. They range from walking tracks to routes for boats and sledges to follow on and through the sea ice. Seasonality is critical. Winter months are better for travelling because the ice is thicker and generally safer but it also brings its own set of challenges. Adjusting for where animals might be found on the edge of the sea ice or the polar plateau is critical to ensuring community survival. Every year, older hunters would share their knowledge and experience with younger community members to ensure that there was a generational transfer of local and regional knowledge of Inuit worlds. Seasonal change coupled with the overall warming of the Arctic, however, makes knowledge transfer precarious in the sense that the year to year endurance of sea ice can never be taken for granted.

Any map of Inuit Nunangat (Homeland of Inuit encapsulating some 50,000 people) starts with the premise that Inuit have distinct homelands occupied by some 53 local communities working across land, sea and ice. There are four major Inuit regions that do not align with the Canadian territories and provinces of Yukon, Northwest Territories, Newfoundland, Labrador

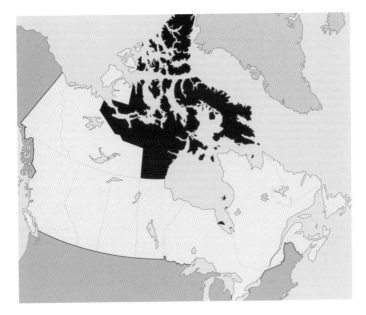

Map of Nunavut, Canada.

and Quebec. The four homelands are Inuvialuit (north of Yukon), Nunavut (a separate and legally recognized territory established in 1999), Nunavik (north of Quebec) and Nunatsiavut (northeast of Newfoundland and Labrador). These northern homelands are found on the northern edge of Canada, where the concentration of sea ice is greatest. Unlike for explorers and travellers past and present, sea ice is a welcome part of Inuit lives. It is literally the foundation for their lives and the features of ice such as ridges, pressure points and fissures are an integral part of their movement, exchange and engagement with other communities both indigenous and Western.

Inuit publicized their 'Inuit Declaration on Sovereignty in the Arctic' in 2009 as a counterpoint to the national governments who were publicly debating future Arctic geopolitics. The Declaration made clear that:

> Inuit live in the vast, circumpolar region of land, sea and ice known as the Arctic. We depend on the marine and terrestrial plants and animals supported by the coastal zones of the Arctic Ocean, the tundra and the sea ice. The Arctic is our home.

It also made clear that Inuit expected to be active partners in any discussions about Arctic resources, sovereignty and stewardship:

> As states increasingly focus on the Arctic and its resources, and as climate change continues to create easier access to the Arctic, Inuit inclusion as active partners is central to all national and international deliberations on Arctic sovereignty and related questions, such as who owns the Arctic, who has the right to traverse the Arctic, who has the right to develop the Arctic, and who will be responsible for the social and environmental impacts increasingly facing the Arctic. We have unique knowledge and experience to bring to these deliberations. The inclusion of Inuit as active partners in all future deliberations on Arctic sovereignty will benefit both the Inuit community and the international community.[16]

The Declaration serves as a form of counter-geopolitics, a deliberate rejection of a long-standing colonial and Cold War legacy imaging the Arctic as a space for Western and Soviet/Russian power projection with little regard for those who call it 'home'.

Future icy geopolitics

How might the world's ice and snow influence and shape geopolitics in the future? Ice and snow have often not fitted into Western geographical imaginations, which have been based on a view of Earth that could ultimately be settled, cultivated and regularized through the administration and management of states. The development of infrastructure in alliance with fixed property ownership is integral to the functioning of nation-states. Often found in remote and unstable areas of the world, ice borders resist those settling and administrative impulses. Borders prove difficult to identify and demarcate in high-altitude and ice-bound regions of nation-states. Boundary markers can and do shift as a consequence of severe weather and dramatic events such as avalanches and earthquakes.

The ice-covered regions of the world, however, have also witnessed innovation in governance. The Antarctic Treaty parties did agree to prohibit mining and mineral exploitation and remain committed to protecting Antarctica's ecosystems and aesthetic values. While the Treaty was demanding, and not straightforward given growing interests in the area's resource value, many would conclude that they would rather have it and its associated legal instruments than not. In the northern latitudes, the intergovernmental forum known as the Arctic Council (since 1996) has committed itself to working closely with indigenous peoples as permanent participants. The recognition of indigenous peoples as the long-term inhabitants of the Arctic is significant, given the long history of colonialism, racism and marginalization experienced by indigenous and aboriginal peoples. There are challenges, of course, but it is significant that 'Arctic states' such as Canada, Russia and the United States and non-Arctic states such as China, Japan, Korea and the UK

Emblem of the
Antarctic Treaty
System.

explicitly recognize in the Arctic Council and elsewhere that Inuit and other native peoples must be consulted, engaged with and, in the case of many parts of the Arctic, have legitimate land and resource rights.

Finally, future global geopolitical permutations are going to be shaped by the fate of ice and snow. The Arctic, Antarctic, Himalayas and other glacial bodies will determine future sea levels, freshwater supplies and ultimately the limits of human habitation. Mass population movement is a real possibility and low-lying settlements including cities such as London and Miami appear particularly vulnerable. There was a time when humans looked at and experienced ice sheets, oceans, deserts and mountains with awe, fear and dread, believing these extra-ordinary spaces and environments to be encountered only by the brave and fearless. What were once marginal and remote areas in every sense are now anything but, as we can appreciate better their cardinal role in regulating the behaviour of planetary systems of heat–water exchange. The future looks bleak for the survival of ice and snow, with scientists warning of a world punctuated by flooding, water stress and a rising population demanding its share of energy resources, food supply and mobility.

5 Working with Ice

Ice and snow are valuable commodities. Without the two, ski resorts would be out of business. Before the advent of modern freezing, the ice trade was an integral part of the everyday life of many urban citizens in major cities such as London, New York and colonial Bombay (Mumbai). Military personnel have used ice and snow as an opportunity to test themselves and equipment in cold-weather operations. Cold-weather technologies have also been critical to shipping operators, eager to operate efficiently and safely through the ice-infested waters of the Great Lakes, the Baltic, the Southern Ocean, and the maritime passages to the north of Canada, Greenland, the United States and Russia. Finally, ice has also proved productive for other sorts of tourist activities, from ice skating to snow festivals and sculpture parks such as the long-standing Sapporo Snow Festival in Japan.

Far from being simply a cold substance to play with, ice was big business in the nineteenth century.[1] This was a fact that unsettled the great American wilderness writer Henry David Thoreau, as he reflected on what scores of Irish workers were extracting from Walden Pond and later Spy Pond in Massachusetts. Working during the bitter winter of 1846, Thoreau watched with amazement as thousands of tons of lake ice were extracted and packaged up for delivery elsewhere. Ice was being pillaged and sold. By chance, Thoreau had witnessed the brutal efficiency of the Tudor Ice Company at work, serving markets in the United States and all over the world. By the nineteenth century, ice was a global commodity and integral to modern urban

development and the movement and preservation of perishable goods. Without elemental refrigeration, our world would have looked and felt quite different. It would have also tasted different. As Thoreau noted in *Walden*, 'The sweltering inhabitants of Charleston and New Orleans, of Madras and Bombay and Calcutta, drink at my well.'[2] Ice was no longer the exclusive preserve of the wealthy, and like any other commodity rising demand spurred on those charged with its exploitation and delivery to emerging markets.

Ice harvesting in Spy Pond, Massachusetts, United States, in 1852.

Ice trade

We take for granted now that most modern homes possess a fridge and freezer, with a capability to preserve and manufacture ice on demand. Seventy years ago, however, it was common for householders to preserve their perishable foods and milk via iceboxes, which were made up of river and/or lake ice placed in a sealed container. Harvested in the colder extremes of the United States, residents of major cities such as New York were supplied by lake and river ice importers. The industry was a profitable one and one man in particular was inspirational in its creation and expansion, the Boston-based nineteenth century entrepreneur Frederic Tudor. He formed a view that surplus ice in frozen New England was simply being wasted and could instead be sent to those in more moderate climes who would wish to use it to preserve food, chill drinks and for medicinal purposes such as 'cooling' feverish patients. Using ice harvested in northern New England, Turner developed a national and international ice-export business, serving customers in New York, Martinique, Bombay and Rio de Janeiro. The first exporting venture to Martinique did not end well: wrapped in straw, the lake ice survived the journey but melted on the docks of the Caribbean island because there were no suitable storage facilities.

Being an entrepreneurial fellow, and not deterred after the Martinique disaster, Tudor invested in storage units in destination ports and found new ways to pack and transport cut ice with the assistance of sawdust. Once storage units and preservation techniques were established and settled upon respectively, trading networks expanded to other American cities in the South, such as Charleston and New Orleans, and in the Caribbean, including Cuba and Jamaica. Once delivered, Tudor was eager to promote his product, including in bars, where bar staff were encouraged to offer their customers whiskey, rye and gin with ice. By 1825 an increasingly confident Tudor was examining ways to increase the extraction of lake ice from his supply areas in New England. He joined forces with explorer and inventor Nathaniel Wyeth, who revolutionized the ice industry by introducing a horse-drawn ice-cutting machine. Ice axes and saws were no longer needed and the back-breaking work of previous years was swept aside. After cutting through lake ice, workers armed with iron bars would extract large blocks and then deposit them on carriages in order to be transported elsewhere. Because the blocks of ice were standardized in terms of size, the company was able to treat ice in a similar manner to the modern container industry – economies of scale were easier to secure because of uniformity and better preservation techniques, which enabled American lake ice to sail for weeks on ships and reach its destination in India still intact and ready for use. The New England ice created something of a stir in India, and proved very profitable for Tudor and his Tudor Ice Company. By the mid-1850s, around 150,000 tons of ice a year were leaving Boston Harbor and voyaging to India, China and Japan. Tudor was a very rich man by the end of his life.[3]

In the United Kingdom, the nineteenth-century ice harvesting trade was more precarious because lake and river ice was not produced in the same extraordinary quantities as in the United States. Canal and lake ice from the River Thames and other water bodies was irregular and of poor quality, made worse by urban pollution. English country homes such as Petworth House in the South Downs in southern England established ice houses in the eighteenth century and bought 'clean ice' from Scandinavia. Wenham Lake Ice Company, importing ice from Norway in the late 1850s, serviced the needs of wealthier families. Queen Victoria gave the company a royal warrant. Imported ice was stored in ice outhouses, warehouses and even underground caverns by buyers such as the nineteenth-century Swiss-born entrepreneur Carlo Gatti, who developed London's fledgling ice cream industry in the 1860s onwards. Magazines and newspapers began to promote and publicize the nascent ice industry.[4]

The nineteenth-century ice trade transformed the daily lives of citizens, ranging from changing drinking habits to an entirely new way of approaching food itself, including the way in which food and drinks were preserved and stored. Ice blocks paved the way for a global food industry, with perishable products being shipped, stored and consumed in ways that were previously only possible by salting, pickling and desiccation. Transporting 'fresh food' was becoming a reality and the seasonality of food consumption altered as Tudor experimented with transporting apples, butter, cheese and salmon. Ice was circulating around the world, connecting the United States to markets in the Caribbean, East Asia and South Asia. What was remarkable about Tudor was that he took something that was commonplace and persuaded customers worldwide that ice would transform their drinking and eating habits. He was right.

Freezing nations

The nineteenth-century ice trade initiated a growing liking and familiarity with ice in the domestic lives of American citizens. But iceboxes, while useful for storing ice, had limited storage and required lake ice to be replenished. What if it was possible to generate and store ice within one's own home without being dependent on ice traders? Two men made it possible. A Scottish inventor, James Harrison, was the first to make a fridge in 1851, although it was a far cry from the compact machines we take for granted in our houses. Later innovation helped to miniaturize them but Harrison started the chilling/freezing revolution. It was only about 150 years ago that we began to exercise real control over ice formation and storage, after hundreds of years of constructing and maintaining ice houses, ice pits and ice cutting.

Born in New York a few years after Tudor died in 1864, Clarence Birdseye was destined to further revolutionize the ice industry.[5] After training as a biologist, Birdseye became involved in fur trading and spent time in the ice-covered province of Labrador in Canada. Watching local peoples freezing their foods during the winter months, he became increasingly fascinated

Patent design for the Quick Freeze Machine, dated August 1930.

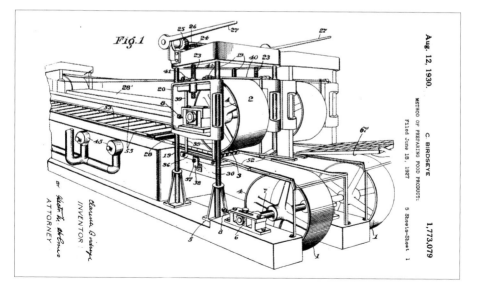

Advert for one of the first mass-produced fridges, the Kelvinator, 1920.

by how ice might be used to freeze foodstuffs such as recently caught fish. After studying the thawing process, he determined that fish and other items such as vegetables appeared to be able to cope with quick freezing in terms of appearance and taste. After some trial and error, Birdseye unveiled what he called the 'Quick Freeze Machine' in 1926, and established a new company, the General Seafood Corporation. It was later acquired by the General Foods Company, which decided to develop the now distinctive Birds Eye trademark.

The Quick Freeze Machine (QFM) was a remarkable innovation, which like the ice trade before it further altered the manner in which food was produced, preserved and distributed. The QFM froze food quickly and placed it in waterproof packaging. After five years of experimentation and improvement, Birdseye filed a patent in June 1927 for a device that was able to freeze and preserve food into ice blocks. The freezing revolution was unfurled, and perhaps all the more remarkable given that Birdseye was far more interested in fur trapping than freezing. He might not have known it at the time but he even got one over on the great physicist Albert Einstein, whose own ideas on refrigeration proved ineffectual.

Winning over the American and later global public depended upon successful marketing and consistent quality. Freezing and frozen foods heralded a highly gendered convenience revolution and the post-war rise in private ownership of fridges and freezers made it possible. The widespread and public availability of summer ice was part of the Cold War cultural frontline, along with domestic appliances such as the freezer, because of their enrolment in claims of American technological superiority. Domestic and supermarket technology allowed American administrations to showcase frozen foods on the one hand and vertiginous towers of canned foods on the other. In the 1950s the u.s.-funded International Congress of Food Distribution organized exhibitions in Italy and Yugoslavia for the express purpose of showing European audiences the diverse array of foodstuffs, including frozen products, available in a typical supermarket.[6]

Modern freezing owes its origins to a white man's observations of Inuit fish-freezing techniques, but some five decades later frozen food was being put to work in a very different context to the one intended by its inventor. In the late 1940s, frozen foods were being touted by American lifestyle magazines as recalibrating the modern family, at least for women and their management of time. Women, imagined as production managers, would be freed from timely fresh food preparation and thus able to demonstrate to their husbands that investing in a freezer was a rational economic decision because it enabled distinct male preferences to be satisfied. Some magazines claimed that freezing might even persuade men to spend more time in the kitchen

because they would be eager to see how ice could be put to work. Where America led, others followed, but far more slowly. In 1948 only about 1–2 per cent of British households owned a fridge and that figure rose to just over 10 per cent in the late 1950s. In comparison, 96 per cent of American households owned fridges by the end of the 1950s.[7]

Frozen foods brochure, 1940s.

By the 1970s, the fridge was a commonplace item for most North American and western European households. But we tend to forget the freezer came far later for many British households in comparison to North American counterparts. The popular British comedy series *Bless this House* (1971–6) had an episode called 'The Frozen Limit', which addressed the impact of a chest freezer on the day to day routines of family life.[8] The episode was first broadcast in January 1976, when having a freezer at home was still quite avant-garde. It helps explain why visitors from North America were constantly surprised at how behind Britain was when it came to frozen food and refrigeration technology. British beer was still too warm and food appeared poorly preserved and stored. It was not until the 1980s, when fridge-freezers were more commonplace, that a growth in the consumption of ice cream, cold drinks and other frozen/fresh goods was facilitated. Newly created supermarkets specializing in frozen items, such as Iceland, which opened its first store in November 1970, brought the 'freezer revolution' into the domestic lives of citizens. By 1980 Iceland had opened over thirty stores, mainly in the north of England and Wales.[9] Meanwhile, in the northern constituencies of Alaska, Canada, Greenland and Russia, consumers to this day pay a high price for importing fresh foods.

Engineering ice

The domestication of ice and the advent of the freezer can be considered integral to a wider engagement with how to build lives around ice and snow. While the post-1945 era witnessed the irresistible rise of the domestic freezer and ice on demand, Cold War science and technology focused attention on how to cope with the vicissitudes of cold weather and better understanding

Freies Gelände
Domaine non contrôlé
Zona non controllata
Off piste areas

Lawinengefahr
Danger d'avalanches
Pericolo di valenghe
Danger of avalanches

Avalanche warning
sign post.

and prediction of ice and snow. Avalanches, permafrost, ice storms and the size and scale of the ice and snow in question were often breathtaking. A large avalanche could release over 200,000 cubic m (7 million cubic ft) of snow, and envelop large areas with a covering of snow extending some 3–4 m (10–13 ft) in depth. They could be even larger, and in May 1970 an avalanche involving snow from Mount Huascarán in Peru slipped off its north-facing slope and travelled 18 km (11 mi.), obliterating everything in its path including 20,000 residents. Some areas were buried under 100 m (330 ft) of ice, mud and rock.

Cold-weather engineering in post-war America and the Soviet Union was the beneficiary of growing geopolitical interest in the Arctic, as engineers were funded and encouraged to better understand thermodynamics, soil mechanics, hydraulics and their cumulative impact on snow and ice and implications for buildings, infrastructures, water supply and civilian and military operations.[10] The management of hazards such as avalanches was one area of real-world impact. Avalanches remain deadly; their capacity to sweep infrastructure away, destroy trees and simply bury people is well recognized. They are also costly to communities and to infrastructure associated with ski resorts and winter-based economies more generally.

Understanding avalanches depended on scientific and technological advances being made about the behaviour of ice, including how snow crystals vary on the basis of temperature, humidity and general atmospheric conditions. Avalanche scientists have determined that the way snowpacks form is critical in determining levels of risk because as snow is compacted the structure of the ice crystals alters. How they alter depends on the role and penetration of surface water and rain, cycles of melting and refreezing, and temperature gradient, which ensures that the snow closest to the ground is warmer than the upper layers of the snowpack. The net result is to bring into contact with one another a mixed assortment of ice akin to an ill-fitting jigsaw puzzle.

Avalanche risk is greatest when snowpacks experience high temperature gradients, regular freeze and melting cycles, and weak rather than compacted layers of snow.[11] Rain and melting snow can play a critical role in allowing the snowpack to overcome the friction holding it in place on the side of a mountain or ice cavity. Depending on where the weakest layer is located within the snowpack, the avalanche will vary in severity. The worst-case scenario, and one that television and films frequently refer to, are the so-called slab avalanches. This is where the snowpack slides over a base layer of snow and detaches itself, before sliding down a slope. Triggers include a sudden and violent change in weather, echoes or human intervention. In the disaster movie *Avalanche* (1978), a crashed helicopter was the trigger, and the action-thriller *Cliffhanger* (1993) depicted a group of criminals launching a deliberate explosive assault on the snowpack in order to generate an avalanche.

For those unfortunate enough to be buried in avalanche snow, it is extremely difficult to escape owing to its sheer weight. James Bond's inflatable jacket designed to engineer an avalanche escape in *The World Is Not Enough* (1999) is the stuff of fantasy. Most people buried in avalanche ice usually have only minutes before being overcome by suffocation. Anyone who survives an avalanche is extremely fortunate and will have had swift access to emergency support. Here are the words of one survivor from an avalanche that hit him in 2003 while on a school trip in Alberta:

> The next thing I remember was being in the snow. I was conscious of what it felt like on my body. I remember the sensation of the slide moving up, of it peaking, and then coming back down and settling. In my head, it was, 'Oh s–t, oh s–t, oh s–t, oh s–t, oh s–t.' At first, the snow was so fluid, but it settled into concrete. I couldn't move anything. I couldn't wiggle my fingers. Which way is up? Which way is down? I couldn't do anything. I couldn't see anything. It was completely dark.[12]

He survived but seven of his party did not. Despite the best efforts of a well-developed rescue infrastructure, the avalanche for some was just overwhelming. There was no escape.

Crown fracture from a slab avalanche in the North Cascades, Washington State, United States.

What avalanche scientists have learnt from studying disasters and modelling the behaviour of ice is that prevention and control depend on careful management. Avalanches are also very costly and disruptive in terms of lives and money. So research has, as with basic glacial research, sought to better understand the snow layers associated with snowpacks and the mechanics of ice. On test slopes, researchers have experimented with deliberately triggering small avalanches to better understand their likely direction of travel. Ice and snow patrols are a regular feature of high-altitude communities, but patrolling can be challenging in remote and barely accessible regions that may be popular with skiers, walkers, snowmobiles, mountaineers and others, including training militaries.

In the early 1950s Austrian and Italian communities in the Alps were hit by a series of deadly avalanches. In the aftermath, European states invested more resources in snowpack observation, intervention including controlled explosions to prevent further snowpack accumulation, regeneration of forestry where possible to act as a natural obstacle to snow and ice flow, and investment in hard engineering solutions including snow retention structures, snow bridges and snow nets. Better signage at ski resorts and recreation areas was also introduced to warn recreational users to avoid high-risk areas and off-piste skiing.

Switzerland is a world leader in avalanche prevention. The first structures were erected in the nineteenth century, but a high-profile series of avalanche disasters in the winter of 1950–51 prompted further investment.[13] Up to 500 km (300 mi.) of steel snow bridges and snow nets held by steel cable were placed on areas judged to be most vulnerable to avalanches. The costs are considerable in terms of maintenance, running to millions of Swiss francs every year, but are judged essential to a country where skiing and winter sports are vital for resort towns such as Davos and Saint Moritz. Advised by the Swiss Institute for Snow and Avalanche Research, the entire country has been mapped and colour-coded on the basis of risk, ranging from red (severe) to blue, yellow and white (low to no risk). The most severe test the country has faced was in February 1999 when seventeen died after an avalanche. The snow protection measures were widely believed to have saved lives and infrastructure. Since the early 1950s it has been estimated that the Swiss authorities have invested around £800 million in avalanche prevention measures.

In the United States, academic centres of excellence in cold-weather engineering including avalanche science were established at universities in Alaska, and across the northern and mountainous states of the country. At the State University of Montana, students can study snow science, while at the University of Washington it is possible to major in cold-regions engineering and learn about snow hydrology and its impact on the state's highways. Military and civil organizations have fully recognized the utility and importance of cold-regions engineering. In 1979 the American Society of Civil Engineers created a Cold Regions Engineering Division, and even earlier, in 1961, the u.s. Army Corp of Engineers established the Cold Regions Research and Engineering Laboratory in New Hampshire. While the stakeholders may vary, the impact of snow and ice on engineering design, construction and resilience cuts across civilian and military constituencies.[14]

The good news for those enjoying the mountains is that avalanche forecasting is now more commonplace and guidelines from agencies such as the u.s. Forest Service National Avalanche

Center warn users of telltale signs of possible trouble such as snow fracture lines and even groaning noises originating from the snowpack. As their website warns: 'Avalanches kill more people on national forests than any other natural hazard. The best way to stay safe is to know the conditions, get the training, carry rescue gear, and stay out of harm's way.'[15]

Fighting on and digging into ice

For the last hundred years, civilian- and military-funded invest-ment has been directed towards gaining a better view and understanding of ice sheets, mountain environments and the watery worlds underneath sea ice and icebergs. The First World War, for example, revealed that it was perfectly possible to con-duct military operations not only on the flat fields of Belgium and France but at altitudes where rock, snow and ice predomin-ated rather than mud, fences and roads. Russian and Austrian troops fought one another in the Carpathian Mountains, Turks and Russians met in the snowy mountains of the Caucasus, and Austrian and Italian troops were locked into a high-altitude conflict along their shared Alpine border.[16] Between May 1915 and November 1918, the Alps and the Italian Dolomites were at the heart of a mountainous confrontation, involving alti-tudes of over 2,000 m (6,500 ft) and sub-zero temperatures and high winds. Both sides invested in infrastructure building and engineering projects, including drilling into the mountains to create artificial caves, trenches and tunnels; and cable cars in order to transport and store supplies necessary for survival in the mountains.

In order to survive such testing conditions, the protagonists developed specialist units with expertise in mountain survival and warfare. Training included skiing, ice climbing and cold-weather medical treatment. Both sides recognized the tactical advantage of occupying higher ground and used explosives to deliberately trigger avalanches and landslides. The most notable event was the Battle of San Matteo in the summer of 1918, when Austrian and Italian troops confronted one another at over

3,600 m (12,000 ft). Both sides shelled the other in their quest to secure the strategically advantageous San Matteo Peak, although it eventually resulted in a short-lived victory for the Austrian forces. Within months Austrian and German forces surrendered but at the time it offered a remarkable illustration of how soldiers and their artillery could operate at high altitudes in a struggle to secure the peak of a mountain that was surrounded by a glacier. In 2004 retreating ice revealed the bodies

Composite image of Italian forces in the Dolomites between 1915 and 1918.

of three Austrian mountain soldiers who had died near the peak
of the mountain.

The onset of the Second World War triggered further
investment in understanding polar and mountain environments
and the advancement of cold regions warfare training. Institutions such as the Scott Polar Research Institute (SPRI) at the
University of Cambridge were important repositories of cold-
weather intelligence, as were the Arctic Institute of North
America, the U.S. Naval Hydrographic Institute, the Canadian
Geographic Branch, and the Defence Research Board (DRB) in
the North American context. After 1945 the SPRI employed scientists such as the Russian-speaking Terence Armstrong, who
was a leading authority on the Soviet Union and its exploitation
of the Soviet Far North. Critically, Armstrong read Russian-
language science and technology reports where they were still
available, and kept abreast of Soviet Arctic science. Navies
needed to know about sea ice forecasting, air forces required a
better understanding of the effects of polar weather on flying,
and armies were preoccupied with the impact of snow and ice

Finnish soldiers
during the Winter
War against the
Soviet Union, 1939.

on critical infrastructure. But as Cold War relations worsened, Soviet scientists were less and less inclined and indeed able to share their sea ice research.

Across the Arctic, snow and ice prevailed for many months, most noticeably in the Russian and North American Arctic, where unlike the Nordic Arctic no Gulf Stream existed to moderate sea and ice temperatures. Cold War intelligence on cold regions was shaped by the experiences of the Second World War. After all, Finland successfully circumvented a Soviet invasion of the country in the 'Winter War' of 1939–40 by attacking Soviet forces using ski-equipped white-clad soldiers. Finnish soldiers became the most skilled exponents of winter warfare, frustrating Soviet forces in 1939–40, and then attacking German army positions in the winter of 1944. Allied and German troops faced one another in Svalbard as both sides sought to secure strategically significant coal mines and weather stations, albeit often frustrated by severe weather and icy conditions.[17]

What two world wars taught combatants and observers alike was that winter warfare demanded investment in specialist training and equipment and sophisticated scientific-technical understanding of the challenges posed by snow and ice. After the Second World War, the United States led the way in examining what was required to train and fight in Arctic, sub-Arctic, cold and mountainous environments. Cold-weather training units were established in Washington State and then the territory of Alaska. In 1948 the Army Arctic School was established at Fort Greely in Alaska in recognition of worsening relations with the Soviet Union and the need to ensure that any troops dispatched to the northern edge of the North American Arctic were trained in mountaineering, skiing and survival techniques. The school was charged with developing cold weather and mountain warfare doctrine, and by 1963, as training provision expanded, a decision was taken to establish the u.s. Army Northern Warfare Training Center at Fort Wainwright in Alaska.[18]

Other branches of the u.s. armed forces were also developing their cold-weather training capabilities and using other cold regions to exercise and train. Notably the u.s. Navy initiated operations in the Arctic and Antarctica called Operation Nanook (1946) and Operation High Jump (1946–7) respectively. The former was smaller and involved six ships engaging in mapping and surveying work off the coastlines of Alaska, Canada and Greenland. The latter was more ambitious and was led by a flotilla of thirteen ships containing nearly 5,000 men and 33 aircraft. High Jump was designed to provide logistic support to the U.S. Antarctic programme and establish a new research station called Little America. Helicopters were used extensively. Operation Windmill (1947–8) was the follow-up operation and cemented a long-standing relationship between the U.S. Navy and U.S. Antarctic science. It had the benefit of ensuring that U.S. naval personnel were regularly exposed to cold-weather conditions in an area of the world that was largely spared the explicit Cold War geopolitical tensions. While geographically remote, all cold-weather military operations have one thing in common – they are heavily photographed and videoed. Even in the 1940s the U.S. Navy wanted to show off their ability to work in these testing environments but, as tensions grew with the Soviet Union, increasingly the photographic and mapping

A U.S. Coast Guard helicopter taking off during Operation High Jump (1946–7).

intelligence gathered by ships, planes and submarines was not being publicly shared.[19]

Navigating sea ice

Another way to practise cold-weather training is to send fighter jets to bomb sea and river ice: a practice usually imagined by novelists rather than air marshals. In the winter of 2015–16, news media reported that Russian fighter pilots were active in the Vologda region of northwest Russia, a major transport hub. su-34 jets were dispatched to attack an ice jam, which was blocking a frozen river. Fearing major flooding following the first signs of late winter melting, local officials hoped that the laser-guided bombs they dropped would destroy the clogged sections of the river. The air force was called in after attempts by two ice-breakers had failed to clear the accumulated river ice. In March 2014 China also deployed a fighter-bomber in order to drop 24 bombs on an ice-clogged Yellow River, which again was blocking access and leading to fears that flooding might result. While ice jams are not uncommon in North America, the use of military planes in Russia and China was a novelty, as u.s. and Canadian operators tend to use Coast Guard assets and heavy construction equipment, including excavators.

For the Soviet Union/Russia, the presence of sea ice and river ice is a major preoccupation. For much of the twentieth century, dealing with sea ice was a strategic priority given the severity of winters, the danger of inland flooding and the sheer scale of the snow-covered northern territories.[20] Informed by Marxist-Leninist ideology, ice and snow were conceptualized as material and cultural obstacles to the progression of a post-revolutionary Soviet Union. The Soviet north, including Arctic territories, were crucial to industrial and resource-led development, and the Northern Sea Route (nsr) stretching from the Bering Strait to the Barents Sea was considered integral to the country's future economic development and geopolitical security. Roads were built, ports opened and labour camps/Gulags established. Convict labour was used to build the White Sea Canal in the 1930s

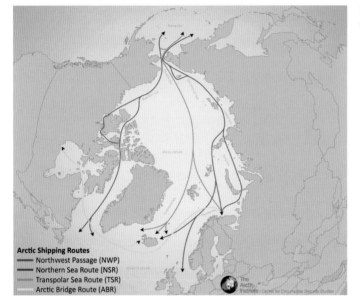

Map of Arctic
shipping routes.

connecting Russian Arctic waters to the Baltic Sea. Stalin's vision
for the Arctic was brutal – nature was to be conquered and ice and
permafrost either annihilated or overcome by Soviet ingenuity.

Before Western scientists focused a more sustained attention on sea ice compared to glaciers and ice sheets, Soviet polar
science led by the Ukraine-born Nikolai Zubov and the State
Institute of Oceanography were world leaders in the 1920s and
'30s.[21] Voyaging four times in the Barents Sea, the waters located
in the northeast regions of Russia, Zubov investigated the interaction between ocean temperatures, seawater mixing and wind
currents in the formation and distribution of sea ice. He was
later appointed secretary of the Russian committee to the Second
International Polar Year (1932–3) and undertook further oceanographic studies of the Russian northern and Arctic waters. His
most famous publication was *Arctic Ice*, published in 1945 in
Russian and translated into English in 1963 by the U.S. Naval
Hydrographic Office. The latter were eager to access Zubov's
thesis about an 'air-ice-water' system and how it might be possible to predict the depth and thickness of sea ice using weather
pressure readings.[22]

As the Second World War brutally revealed, sea ice in the North Atlantic and Barents Sea was a major hazard to shipping and made resupply of the Soviet Union challenging as convoy ships had to evade German U-Boats, which were beneficiaries of ice-covered waters. As Soviet researchers appreciated, sea ice was not uniform in coverage and thickness, as the ice endures shearing, crushing and cracking. As a consequence of this pummelling it becomes uneven and patchwork-like and subject to the vagaries of ocean and wind currents. Predicting sea ice was akin to alchemy, a form of magic only possible by the careful, long-term study of relevant ice-covered seas and oceans. As Zubov recognized, the formation and drift of sea ice was not for the academically and logistically faint-hearted – the sea ice scientist needed to understand ice physics, ocean chemistry and meteorology and be prepared to undertake multiple voyages to the source areas of sea ice.

Understanding the dynamics of Arctic sea ice fed directly into national security planning during the Cold War. Soviet scientists and military officials wanted to predict annual cycles of sea ice formation and dispersal. Navigation and accessibility was

Convict labour was used to construct the White Sea Canal 1931–3.

essential for servicing northern coastal communities but also important for determining the potential movement of civilian and military vessels under and on polar waters. In the Soviet era, the NSR was no longer the stuff of dreams of earlier European explorers such as Sir Hugh Willoughby and Willem Barents in the sixteenth century. By the twentieth century, Russian explorers such as

Soviet Union stamp of the nuclear-powered submarine *Leninsky Komosomo* navigating through sea ice, 1970.

Vitus Bering had explored the northern domain of the country in a series of 'Great Northern Expeditions', including land mapping and hydrographic surveying of northern rivers and coastlines. Ice-breakers joined the fray in the 1920s and '30s and undertook extensive sea ice observations with the blessing of the Chief Directorate of the NSR, led by the ambitious administrator and polar scientist Otto Schmidt. As captain of the doomed ship *Chelyuskin*, which was trapped and destroyed in sea ice in 1932, he was famed for ensuring the survival of the trapped crew and passengers as they awaited eventual rescue.

By 1937 the NSR was served by a string of meteorological stations, ice-breakers and drifting stations (the first being North Pole 1 station) in the Arctic Ocean. High-quality sea ice prediction equated to a sense of operational security and the long-term economic viability of the NSR as a transport route for Soviet exports of timber, fur, coal and fish.

The United States wanted to access better Soviet expertise on sea ice as its own ambitions grew in the North American Arctic from establishing a new airbase in Thule in northwest Greenland to initiating the circumpolar Distant Early Warning system (DEW) in the early 1950s. Sea ice forecasting was essential because most of the equipment and infrastructure being positioned in the high Arctic was transported by ship. Getting stuck not only necessitated delay but fed a geopolitical imagination based on fear: were the Soviets better able to predict sea ice and thus use it to their strategic and tactical advantage? Later, anxiety turned to something more sinister: could the Soviets hide their submarines under sea ice and would U.S. underwater surveillance be sufficiently nuanced to detect enemy submarines in distinction, say, from icebergs and marine mammals, especially whales?

The underwater voyage of the USS *Nautilus* in July–August 1958 was deliberately timed to reassure an American public unnerved by Soviet technological-scientific achievement in space and the Arctic. Leaving the west coast of America, the nuclear-powered submarine became the first to transit the North Pole, after an initial voyage was curtailed by thick sea ice. The voyage was intended to showcase American technology, including a new navigation system designed to enable long-term submerged voyaging and test possible obstacles under the ice. If the Soviets had their ice hero in the form of Nikolai Zubov, the

The Distant Early Warning Line, northern Alaska, United States.

Americans had chief scientist Waldo Lyon, who spearheaded the *Nautilus* operation (Operation Sunshine) from the u.s. Arctic Submarine Laboratory in the balmy climes of San Diego, California.[23] What the American public celebrating the news about the *Nautilus* voyage were not told, however, was that some months earlier in February 1958 American and Soviet ice scientists actually met with Japanese and European colleagues for a conference on Arctic sea ice.[24] Although Soviet participation was not straightforward at the time, the u.s.-hosted conference began to share information on sea ice characteristics, including physical composition, distribution and implications for navigation.

Some of the information collected by the u.s. and Soviet navies during the Cold War on Arctic sea ice and navigation was released gradually to civilian scientists from the 1990s onwards. But there is still tremendous sensitivity towards sea ice research and forecasting in Russia.[25] While the country may be less concerned about u.s. nuclear submarines and a possible nuclear attack (and vice versa), the NSR is attracting increasing commercial attention as operators highlight the vaunted savings in terms of sailing time and distances compared to conventional trade routes via the Suez Canal. The journey from the Dutch port of Rotterdam to the Japanese port of Yokohama is thousands of kilometres shorter if the NSR is chosen. With reports of sea ice thinning and in retreat, Russia is promoting the NSR as a commercial route for the future because it can charge operators transit fees and at the same time reinforce its sovereign authority over the waters north of the Russian Federation.

Longer term, however, Russia's future economic development is dependent on resource extraction in the Arctic and the transportation of liquefied natural gas to Asian and European markets via the NSR. Sea ice forecasting remains as crucial as ever to Russia, especially as the operational season extends only from July to November at present. Regardless of new technologies, including the use of ship-launched drones to provide real-time sea ice forecasting, navigating through sea ice remains precarious and as potentially challenging now as it did for nineteenth-century explorers. What has changed, markedly, is that scientists and coast guards share more readily than they once did insights about Arctic sea ice. Arctic states and the International Maritime Organization (IMO) recognize that they share a mutual interest in ensuring safe shipping. Shrinking sea ice does not mean that sea ice no longer represents an operational challenge for ship navigation, stability or propulsion.

Without proper guidelines and regulations that anticipate the impact of future climate change on industrial development and resource use (such as commercial fisheries, cruise traffic and shipping), local communities may become more vulnerable to changing conditions. The development of the IMO 'Polar Code' (which came into force in January 2017) for Arctic shipping is an example of a proactive form of adaptation to changing ocean conditions. The Polar Code, by setting standards for safety and reporting, is the first set of internationally recognized guidelines for the construction and operation of ships in ice-covered Polar waters.[26]

6 Sport, Leisure and Pleasure on Ice

Winter pastimes such as skiing, bowling, skating, ice driving, tobogganing and even snowball fights reveal that living and working with ice and snow have not always been a matter of life and death. Adapting to snow and ice led to sporting innovation: as recreational skiers know, there was once a time when nobody snowboarded on the slopes. Many people enjoy the experience of travelling over ice, feeling ice and playing games on ice. In some cases, participants might be far removed from environments where snow and ice are either permanent or seasonal realities. Skiing on dry ice runs might be a good example of how it is possible to have the sensation of sliding on ice even if the ice and snow are artificial in nature.[1]

In this chapter, we consider the most famous winter sport – skiing – and then address wider sporting cultures on ice and snow. We have, since 1925, encouraged and supported our fellow humans to be the best skiers, skaters and the like at the Winter Games, with the latest being held at the Russian resort of Sochi in 2014. Sport also complements recreational activities on ice and snow, such as ice fishing on frozen lakes and rivers. Finally, our survey will turn to tourists, and the lure of ice sculptures and ever-larger festivals celebrating the intrinsic beauty of ice rather than visiting ice-covered regions per se. There is now a medley of events and festivals involving ice, including a World Ice Art Championship, the Harbin International Ice and Snow Sculpture Festival in China, an Ice Fishing Festival in Korea, the International Festival of Ice Sculptures in Russia, the Ice

Music Festival in Norway, the New Zealand IceFest and the long-established Sapporo Snow Festival in Japan, which started in 1950. For the intrepid and reasonably well heeled, it is also possible to enjoy the comforts of ice hotels, such as the world's first such establishment built at Jukkasjärvi, in northern Sweden, alongside an ice church.[2] Adapting to ice has been fun and enjoyable for many humans.

Having fun on ice has also come at a proverbial price, however. Ice skating, skiing and ice fishing have sometimes ended disastrously. In January 1867 a frozen lake in Regent's Park in central London gave way after hundreds of skaters took to the ice. Scores of skaters fell into the freezing water and some forty drowned because of the weight of their skates and clothing. An unregulated and hugely popular pastime proved fatal and in the aftermath the lake itself was drained so that it had a depth of

Ice church,
Jukkasjärvi, Sweden.

167

only 1.2–1.5 m (4–5 ft) deep rather than 4 m (12 ft). Unbeknown to the skaters, park keepers had been creating artificial gaps in the ice in order to support the resident overwintering wildlife. It all seems a far cry from Gerard Manley Hopkins's 1877 poem 'Windhover', which compares the ice skater to the falcon as floating or moving effortlessly over the ice while enjoying a sure sense of direction and accompanying poise.

ESKIMO GIRL ON SNOW SHOES, ALASKA.

COPYRIGHT 1907 BY CASE & DRAPER.

Eskimo girl on snow shoes, Alaska, United States.

Danger is not unique to ice skating. Skiers have been consumed by avalanches, ice fishermen have fallen through fishing holes, and people and their vehicles attending winter festivals have been consumed by freezing water. In February 2016 fifteen cars went through lake ice during the Lake Geneva Winterfest. Thankfully, no one was hurt in the incident.

Skiing

The first recorded use of skis was in the Palaeolithic era, some 12,000 years ago, in the Xinjang Uygur region in northwest China.[3] They were developed by a distinct group of Mongolians called Tuvan. In 2005 archaeologists in Handerte, Mongolia, found a rock painting that they believe shows humans on ancient skis, clearly designed to help local communities move around the deep snow and ice characteristic of the region. A distinct ski-making tradition still exists in the region, using spruce as the plank with strips of thick horsehair attached to the base to aid in gliding over the snow and ice. With a snow depth of at least 1–2 m (3–6 ft) per season, the skis represent a vital source of mobility in an environment where snow and ice can endure for seven months of the year. Hunting moose remains a popular winter activity and the horsehair-lined skis are particularly prized for their ability to allow hunters not only to glide downhill but to climb up slopes and hills to chase their prey. Villages around the Altay Valley region are frequently cut off from motorized transport during the long winter months. Strikingly, the design and application of the ski has not changed for centuries.

Most Inuit hunting was carried out over sea ice so skis were less useful and snowshoes were used relatively modestly when travelling over ice towards open water.[4] Deep snow tended to be found in more mountainous and sheltered areas inland rather than coastal provinces. However, Native American tribes used snowshoes more than skis. Taking inspiration from the animals they encountered, including winter hares such as the aptly named Snowshoe Hare, North American tribes such as the Huron and

Algonquin developed designs that were intended to resemble paw prints of animals such as the hare, bear and beaver embedded in the snow. Often oversized in design, sometimes as long as 2–3 m (6–10 ft), the snowshoe design used wood, rawhide and animal skin and bone to tie the structures together.

Pre-dating the wheel, it is no exaggeration to say that the ski and snowshoe were essential elements in human mobility and survival in extreme environments. Across northern Europe, North America and Asia, there is archaeological evidence of skis and snowshoes being widely used as a consequence of the regular and ultimately predictable demands of winter months, and the unrelenting need to discover new food sources and territories. In 2013 in Russia, scientists discovered a rock drawing some 4,000 years old depicting a group of hunters on skis pursuing a fast-moving elk. Being a good slider was key to being a good hunter and survivor.

This global prehistory of skiing is not one that is always appreciated by European observers, who tend to start their accounts of skiing with ancient Norway and rock drawings that suggest men (and deities) were gliding over the ice some 4,000 to 5,000 years ago. Ski-related debris was also discovered in a peat bog in the north of Sweden and dated to around 4,500 years ago. Other finds were made in caves in Norway and Finland, identified as around 3,200 years old, showing, quite reasonably, that Nordic herders, hunters and trappers used skis. Norse storytelling suggests that people skied for fun as well. The word 'ski' comes from the ancient Norse word *skíð*, meaning 'a billet or chunk of wood', and the ski was embellished in Norse legend through the exploits of Skadi, goddess of the ski and snowshoe. Living in ice-covered mountains, and a lover of the wilderness, she was depicted and imagined as a tall and fierce huntress who was happiest when equipped with skis or snowshoes and armed with her hunting weapons.[5]

Modern-day skiing, for most, remains decidedly recreational rather than grounded in activities such as hunting and fishing, and exploratory or military planning. Skiing grew in popularity in the nineteenth century, and was popular with a new generation of enthusiasts who helped to pioneer the ski holiday. By 1903 British figures such as Sir Henry Lunn, the founder of the travel company Lunn Poly, had introduced well-heeled customers to the idea of the ski package holiday.[6] A devout man, Lunn took ski parties to Swiss hotels and argued that winter sports were an integral part of spiritual and physical well-being. Having formed the Public Schools Alpine Club, Lunn was later instrumental in establishing the Alpine Ski Club in 1908, designed to bring together ski enthusiasts. For Lunn and his contemporaries, such as the mountaineer Sir Martin Conway, skiing brought one into intimate contact with nature, especially in Alpine environments; British skiers, unlike their Nordic peers, adopted downhill rather than cross-country styles. They quickly became accustomed to sliding down well-maintained mountain slopes on bound skis, as opposed to their Nordic counterparts who combined skating, running and walking motions with looser bindings. Ski technology also changed, allowing skiers to take advantage of cambered edges, adjustable bindings and metal edges designed to get a better purchase on icy slopes. As ski construction altered, so skiers discovered they could master bumps, ridges and different sorts of snow.

Ski terminology developed and evolved to distinguish between powdery and sticky snow, moguls and bumps, graduation of slopes and skier experience, as well as the social rituals associated with après-ski. And all of this has occurred against the backdrop of the commercial development of a global ski industry and mountain tourism that includes other recreational activities such as skidoos or mechanized sledges and snowboarding. As skiing became more popular, so the dictates of fashion became ever more prominent as specialist clothing, equipment and the lure of exclusive resorts shaped the popular cultural imagination. Walt Disney released a cartoon film, *The Art of Skiing*, in 1941, and introduced young audiences for the first time to downhill skiing courtesy of Goofy the Dog. By the 1950s and '6os, it was possible to speak of a 'ski-set', with an array of glamorous, famous and rich people such as Bridget Bardot photographed on the slopes of resorts in France and Switzerland. Goofy they were not. Meanwhile, a young Queen Elizabeth II knighted Henry Lunn in 1952 for his 'services to skiing'.

European Alpine resorts in the twenty-first century are increasingly dependent on artificial snow.[7] The Alps are facing a warming trend that is greater than lowland Europe with predictions that the snowline will have fallen by the end of the century, with some 300–400 m (1,000–1,300 ft) lost from the current levels. In Switzerland, the epicentre of the European ski industry, permanent ice will be a precious commodity as glaciers and mountain snow continue to retreat. Downhill skiing demands far more snow and ice coverage than cross-country skiing, but the physical and imaginative geography of the Alps invites speed and exhilarating descent while surrounded by majestic glaciers and mountains. Ski tourism in the European Alps is responsible for nearly 200 million skier visits per year. For many mountain resorts, 80–90 per cent of their economy is reliant on tourism, and uncertain winters with corresponding implications for snow

Howelsen Ski Resort, Colorado, United States.

and ice formation have meant that local authorities have had to either diversify what they offer visitors or invest in artificial snow production. Another strategy has been to introduce snow farming, where old snow is stored and supplemented with new and artificial snow.

European ski resorts are not the only ones facing challenges posed by climate change and unreliable snow levels. Thirty-eight out of fifty u.s. states have snow economies and states such as Colorado were pioneers in making money from winter sports.[8] The first ski area in the country was opened in 1915 at Howelsen Hill in that state. The industry is worth around $8 billion and the National Ski Association estimates that over 200,000 jobs are dependent on ski visits by Americans and international visitors. There are regional variations, with snowboarding being particularly popular in the Great Lakes states of Minnesota, Michigan and Wisconsin. But snow loss is a real problem for resorts in Colorado and western America and often contrasts, paradoxically, with news that major cities have been hit by record amounts of snow and bombarded with violent ice storms. A snowboard world cup event in 2015 at the popular Squaw Valley, California, had to be cancelled because of lack of snow. And analysts predict that Colorado could lose thousands of jobs and up to $1 billion in revenues in the next few years if skiers and snowboarders stay away from snow-starved resorts. So ski resorts will have to adapt further or find alternatives.[9]

Sport on ice

Adapting to ice and snow has, as the history of skiing demonstrates, involved all sorts of mutations, many of which were not motivated by basic needs such as the pursuit of shelter, food and trade. Winter sports are tremendously popular and it would be hard to appreciate the popular cultures of countries like Canada, for example, if you didn't factor in the role of 'hockey' (never 'ice hockey') in everyday life. Former Prime Minister Stephen Harper was famously hockey-mad and it has often informed an idealization of what the Canadian man should be like – rugged, outdoorsy and competent with an ice hockey stick (and in the summer months armed with a canoe paddle). In a country dominated for months by the presence of ice and snow, hockey has been a staple feature of Canadian life since the 1870s. Montreal was the birthplace of Canadian hockey, boasting the first team, and the first major competition was held at the 1883 Montreal Ice Carnival. A Canadian innovation, the ice-smoothing tractor called the Zamboni, designed by the Canadian Frank Zamboni, contributed in the post-1945 period to a highly engineered approach to ice hockey. As the game became professionalized, the management of the ice also became subject to innovation and intervention.

The international diffusion of ice hockey to other parts of the world began in the United States and then spread to Europe. Played mainly outdoors initially, the game transferred indoors into sporting stadia with artificial ice rather than open areas covered with ice surrounded by snow barriers. Canada and the United States in the interwar period developed a National Hockey League and, over the decades, hockey grew in popularity as the number of teams admitted expanded along with the star power of leading players. Among professional sports, ice hockey was perhaps the one that became most embroiled in

Two Zambonis operating in an ice hockey rink.

'Miracle on the Ice' – the USA–USSR ice hockey match at the 1980 Winter Olympics, Lake Placid, New York.

Cold War geopolitical rivalries, as Canada, the United States, the Soviet Union, Czechoslovakia, Finland and Sweden battled it out on the ice. Notably the so-called 'Miracle on the Ice' in 1980 witnessed a stunning U.S. victory over the Soviet Union, champions at the previous six Winter Olympic Games. The American team later won gold in the final against Finland.

Ice hockey was one of the original sports to be represented at the Chamonix Winter Games in 1924, where 258 athletes competed from sixteen national Olympic committees in sixteen events. Originally called the 'International Winter Sports Week', it was rebranded as the Olympic Winter Games in 1926. Charles Jewtraw of the USA was the first Olympic champion in the history of the Winter Games. Fast forward to the 2014 Winter Olympics Games in Sochi, Russia, a controversial event hosted by a nation widely condemned for its role in Ukraine's political instability, and its military intervention following the recent Revolution; there were widespread allegations of corruption surrounding the games and fears that there was insufficient snow to host the sports. It was reported that the Sochi Games cost around $51 billion, surpassing the estimated $12 billion comfortably.

There were over 2,800 participants for 98 events, including snow-boarding and bobsleigh, from 88 national Olympic committees, and with new participants Paraguay and Zimbabwe.

As part of a wider promotion of Arctic circumpolar identities, with a particular emphasis on northern and indigenous communities, the 2010 Arctic Winter Olympics was initiated in Canada. With 2,000 participants taking part from Alaska, northern Canada, Greenland and the Russian and Nordic Arctic, the Arctic Winter Olympics is held every two years, with the latest being in Greenland in 2016. What we might reasonably ask about such sporting initiatives is the hidden environmental and financial costs. Even the Arctic Winter Games, while laudable, divert precious resources from more everyday priorities and place stresses on communities with limited infrastructure and housing capacities.

Recreation on ice

Having fun on the ice has been of great importance to many people who live with seasonal ice. The range of activities that have captured the imagination of residents and holidaymakers alike encompasses mobility (ice skating and tobogganing) and immobility (ice fishing). In Canada, the toboggan is a quintessential element of many childhoods, and echoes the recorded observations of how early settlers and even more significantly indigenous peoples moved around the vast ice-covered land. Handmade toboggans were fashioned from wood, such as larch and pine, and tied into a cross-bar structure designed to facilitate mobility. They might be close to 3 m (10 ft) in length and narrow in width. The narrowness was designed to allow users, wearing snowshoes or skis, to attach themselves to the toboggan.

The toboggan was developed to aid and abet transport and commercial activities like fur trapping and hunting in the Canadian north. By the late nineteenth century, it had become associated with leisure and entertainment. In 1881 the Montreal Tobogganing Club was established, holding competitions throughout the city. For the wealthier citizens of Canadian cities like Toronto and Quebec City, tobogganing was considered highly fashionable. In 1935 a toboggan run was built close to the Fairmont Chateau Frontenac Hotel in Quebec City. Open between December and March each year, the three-chute run still operates and stretches for a quarter of a mile downhill.

In places like the u.s. state of Minnesota and Nordic countries like Finland, where the lakes created by past glacial action host a great deal of lake ice, ice fishing thrives. In the coldest areas of Minnesota, for example, lakes can be frozen for eight to nine months per year. In the nineteenth century, Scandinavian emigrants introduced ice fishing as pioneers built their outhouses over the frozen lakes. Fishing for around a week at a time, the overwhelmingly male preoccupation was intensely homosocial, given the cramped living and working conditions.

The play *Nice Fish* (2016), co-written by Mark Rylance and Louis Jenkins, aims to recreate childhood experiences of ice fishing on a lake in Minnesota. Two old friends, Eric and Ron, spend the day musing about their friendship and their lives

Tourist brochure illustrating Montreal's tobogganing runs, 1926.

MONTREAL *for Hospitality*

MONTREAL Winter Attractions

MONTREAL *for Healthy Sports*

Park Slide on Mount Royal

ahead. Sitting on their upturned buckets, the men fish with their specially shortened ice fishing poles. They are designed to be placed through a small hole (around 15–30 cm/6–12 in. in diameter) in the ice and taken out safely when a catch is detected. What the play trades on is something that the American poet Ralph Burns also explored in his poem 'Fishing in Winter': the idea that the elemental qualities of ice, fog and cold nourish and provoke memories of past lives and relationships made manifest in frigid environments.

Ice Fishing, popular also in Estonia, Norway, Iceland, Canada and Russia, has more recently witnessed the introduction of underwater sonar technologies to improve fish detection. But for purists, a short pole, fishing spear or simple line with hook is still the preferred approach. Ice fishing competitions are also popular. In the United States, Michigan and Minnesota host annual competitions which can bring nearly 40,000 people to the lakes. Houghton Lake in Michigan is particularly popular. Elsewhere, in Finland, for example, a national championship is held every year in February and attracts several thousand to the lakes. In 2016 it was reported that fishermen were having to drill over 60 cm (2 ft) into the lake ice in order to make contact with the water underneath. In the past, around 5–6,000 people were reported at such competitions, and there may be signs that younger Finns are less wedded to the activity, just at a time when Finnish tourist authorities are marketing the practice to international visitors.

Beyond the highly publicized worlds of skiing and ice skating, tobogganing and ice fishing are integral to northern cultures. But they are not unique to western cultures. In China, there is the annual Chagan Lake Ice Fishing and Hunting Culture Tourism Festival. The Chagan Lake in northeast China is one of the largest freshwater lakes, and ice fishing has existed there for thousands of years. But unlike the small-scale ice fishing imagined in plays like *Nice Fish*, the festival witnesses several hundred skilled fishermen operating nets under the ice and hauling tons of carp to the surface. Using an adapted Mongolian fishing technique, thousands of visitors watch the

Ice fishing on Lake
Harriet, Minnesota.

local community perform an array of religious dances, singing and praying. The festival, lasting from December to January, has become an important and lucrative event for the local economy.

Ice tourism

Ice tourism in the form of ice festivals is now firmly established in many countries, including China, Canada and the Nordic states. The most notable ice festivals are Sapporo Snow Festival, Fairbanks World Ice Art Championship, Quebec City Winter Carnival, Norway's Ski Festival and the Harbin International Ice and Snow Festival. The oldest continuous ice festival is the one hosted at Sapporo, which began somewhat modestly in 1950. At that time six snow statues were constructed by local students, but the event proved surprisingly popular, with thousands drawn to the spectacle. In more recent times, some 2 million people visit the northern Japanese city to see the snow and ice sculptures made in February each year. Their scale varies from small and compact to the truly enormous, including at the 2017 festival an enormous ice bust of Donald Trump and a 17-m (56-ft) Eiffel Tower.

The most notable ice festival is the one held in China's northern city of Harbin, which is one of the coldest places in the country. Since the mid-1980s, the ice and snow festival, which

runs over January and February, has become bigger each year, drawing in over 1 million visitors in 2017. Such is its size that thousands of workers are employed in late November and December to retrieve and cut blocks from the Songhua River. The river ice forms the building blocks for around 7,000 artists and sculptors to create replica buildings and towers, such as Rome's Colosseum. Other creations in 2017 included ice castles, trains and famous buildings, usually decked out with thousands of lights.

International Ice and Snow Festival in Harbin, China.

What makes the festival notable – apart from size and spectacle – is that ice carving is part of the city's history. From at least the sixteenth century, fishermen were known for carving ice lanterns out of river ice from the Songhua River. Within the carved ice blocks fishermen would place candles in their improvised lanterns. Over time, ice lanterns grew in popularity and local families began to hang decorated and festive lanterns outside their homes during the winter months. In 1963 the local government in Harbin organized their first Ice Lantern Festival in order to celebrate this form of ice sculpture. Banned during the Cultural Revolution (1966–76) because of its perceived frivolity, the festival did not make a reappearance until the early 1980s. Given the annual boost to the city's economy, it would be difficult to imagine such cancellations in the near future. Globally, ice festivals continue to garner popularity and stretch across the world as cities and countries seek to capture their share of visitors.

7 Adapting to Ice

Studies suggest that people, animals and plants living in high-altitude environments such as the Andes, Tibet and the Rocky Mountains, where snow and ice are semi-permanent, have adapted physiologically and environmentally to colder and thinner air, to less fertile soils and extremes of weather. In Tibet, for example, scientists discovered that a majority of Tibetans had a very particular gene called EGLNI, developed over thousands of years, which makes their bodies better able to cope with a lower oxygen content and thus avoid the problems typical for others such as altitude sickness.[1] Many members of the Tibetan and other mountainous communities in central Asia are yak herders. The yak, a member of the cattle family, is extraordinarily adapted to the cold and ice, with thick fur, enlarged heart and lungs, and the ability to survive up to 6,000 m (20,000 ft) above sea level. Given its importance to herding economies, it is perhaps not surprising that it is found in Tibetan history, festivals and mythology because of its standing as a food and milk source and ingredient of local medicine. While glacial and permafrost loss due to warming is disruptive, Chinese-led grazing-control policies coupled with infrastructural development are blamed for the degradation of summer pastures that are essential for nomadic yak-herding communities.

New research on snow and ice is increasingly focused on adaptation and change or perhaps simply loss and diminution. The Arctic Council's Snow, Water, Ice and Permafrost Assessment (SWIPA, 2011) is a case in point.[2] Scientists are asking how

A yak in the Nepalese Himalayas.

a changing Arctic environment will respond to seawater and freshwater ice thinning, shorter ice seasons, snow cover reduction and increasing frequency of coastal erosion due to winter storms no longer being isolated by the protective barrier of multi-year ice. Variability will remain. There will continue to be some winter seasons where ice and snow are more prevalent than others. While adaptation has been a long-standing feature of life on and under the ice, the adaptive capacity and resilience of human and non-human communities will depend on physical, biological, economic and societal interactions. What we do know is that Arctic ice and snow perform a regulatory role for the global climate system: they reflect heat back into the atmosphere but when we reduce that ice and snow cover it becomes a sink for heat, and melting permafrost will lead to methane release as plant matter thaws out in vast areas of tundra. The scale of potential change and effect is both intensely local for those who live and work there but also global in its ramifications.

Environmental change and adaptation are of concern to other flora and fauna who also call ice and snow home, including smaller species such as algae, moss and lichen; and iconic animals such as the snow leopard, Arctic fox, albatross, polar bear, whale, penguin and seal. In recent years, detailed oceanographic and biological research has shown that forms of life thrive in the most surprising of places in the frigid habitats of polar waters, glacial bodies and even the underside of sea ice and icebergs. Micro-organisms live in the top few metres of the Earth's ice and, depending on their colour and composition, they play a part in shaping the albedo of that body of ice. Glacial physics and ecology turn out to be shaped by microbes and their efforts to survive in a hostile environment.

Often described as a frigid wasteland, the Antarctic including the Southern Ocean is anything but. There may only be two flowering plants in Antarctica (the Antarctic hair grass and Antarctic pearlwort), which are found in the milder Antarctic Peninsula and South Orkneys, but there are more than two hundred species of lichen and a hundred species of moss scattered around the coastlines and areas of exposed rock. And that is only considering contemporary Antarctica. Fossil evidence (ferns, coal and trees) reveals that the past climate and ecology was very different and closer in character to both tropical and temperate environments.

But adapting to ice and snow remains challenging, and we finish this book with a look at what happens when it becomes too much, even overwhelming. Avalanches are a hazard, but what happens when the infrastructure of our modern, networked and predominantly urban lives fails to cope with winter storms, heavy snowfall, freezing fog and extreme ice? The most awful ice storms that have hit North America merged a lethal cocktail of snow falls, ice accumulation, strong winds and freezing fog that sheered power lines, downed trees, besieged public transport and water-supply systems, and left exhausted communities in darkness, immobile and without heating. In January 1998 the 'Great Ice Storm' hit southern Canada and northeast America, and left millions without power for days and in some cases weeks. Canadian and American military personnel and national guards mobilized, and national emergencies were declared in both countries. Remarkably only 35 fatalities were recorded.[3]

Living on and with ice

The capacity of humans to cope with snow and ice has depended, historically, on three factors – the ability to travel on ice and through polar waters, to stay dry and warm, and to cope with the vicissitudes of cold weather including windburn, snow blindness, dehydration, frostbite and comparative social isolation. What the SWIPA Assessment warns of, however, is that the scale of recent change is disrupting community and infrastructural resilience. The lifestyle and health of Arctic residents are made precarious due to unreliable sea ice and capricious weather. Sea ice hunting becomes more dangerous, and the safety of groundwater drinking supplies is undermined. If traditional indigenous knowledge becomes less relevant in a warming Arctic then there will be fewer opportunities for younger people to become hunters, fishermen and herders. Moving Inuit to residential schools and urban housing environments had very mixed results, as many struggled to adapt to a very different everyday life.[4]

Indigenous peoples living in the Arctic have adapted to the prevailing conditions. They have devised social and cultural codes as well as new technologies to manage everyday life. Resilience is integral to people's livelihoods and conflict resolution remains vital in communities that might be extremely remote and cut

Blok P, the largest residential building at one stage in Nuuk, Greenland.

off from other settlements because of a lack of infrastructure or inclement weather. The adaptive process has therefore required native peoples to devise mechanisms for resolving disputes over hunting and the distribution of food, including using song-duels where protagonists had to sing, dance and entertain the community rather than physically fight one another.[5] What made conflict resolution vital was living in close proximity to one another. Living in igloos, from the Inuit word *igluit*, refers not only to traditional snow-houses but to other houses made out of canvas, wood and brick. In Greenland, the igloo might be a smaller structure made out of ice and designed to offer shelter to the hunter operating at the extreme margins of the sea ice. Whatever the size, a shortage of permanent housing is common in indigenous communities, which can then exacerbate further family and communal tension.

For hunting and longer-term survival, Inuit and other indigenous peoples learned over generations to interpret and predict snow and ice, and to make sense of how air and water currents will alter sea ice, snowdrifts and the likely habitats of animals such as seals, Arctic char and reindeers that were being hunted, fished and managed.[6] A careful reading of the landscapes and seascapes of the Arctic was, at times, a matter of life and death. Falling through ice could and did lead to drowning, and all Inuit hunters, however good their skills, fear a chance encounter with polar bears. Huskies often not only provided companionship for Inuit but helped to alert individuals and community members to the presence of polar bears. Having a close relationship to land, ice and water is integral to Inuit; a lack of access to those traditional food resources has been blamed for undermining community vitality, and a worrying prevalence of suicide among young native men in particular. Mitigation and adaptation to changing patterns of ice is critical to many northern communities in the Arctic region.

While the Soviets and Americans were preoccupied with better sea-ice forecasting during the Cold War, native peoples in the Arctic have over the generations also developed their own forecasting systems. As North American military authorities sought greater knowledge of ice and snow, indigenous peoples were in many cases being forced off the land and resettled in sedentary communities far away from traditional hunting and fishing grounds. Young native peoples were being educated in so-called residential schools with disastrous consequences in terms of their health and well-being. Young people were denied the opportunity to learn from their elders about traditional lifestyles and their detailed knowledge of ice, sea and snow. This led to increased incidence of abuse, self-harm, depression and suicide.

For those who remained in situ, native communities understood that sea ice was not just a platform for hunting and travel but an essential element in defending coastal communities from winter storms. While Western scientists began to better understand the ecological services provided by sea ice, traditional indigenous knowledge long recognized, through language and practice, that the ice was essential to communal food security and well-being. Local knowledge, enriched by animist beliefs and spiritual values, was also repeatedly tested and evaluated by real-world experience and adjusted where it made sense because of variations in ice depth and thickness, snow cover extent, and extent of melting and flooding. Experimentation and reflection was an approach that also found favour with militaries eager to learn adaptive techniques from indigenous peoples.

What geophysical scientists and anthropologists have learnt from native peoples is that traditional indigenous knowledge embodied in the memories and experiences of elders and experienced hunters is extraordinarily place-sensitive and detailed regarding local topographies and prevailing weather. Accessing indigenous knowledge has proven beneficial to non-native visitors and at times posed a challenge to national and global assessments of Arctic sea ice and fauna. Local hunters have advised scientists on where early and late access to sea ice is possible, the location of stable ice platforms where research might be possible, and errors and mistakes in prevailing non-indigenous maps. In Alaska, Inupiat and Yupik Eskimo communities have proven invaluable as sources of information on the whale population. Having hunted whales for hundreds of years, the communities have developed a keen interest in monitoring numbers of Bowhead whales and making assessments about sustainable hunting. Native knowledge of whale behaviour drew attention to the disruption caused to animal migratory patterns by seismic surveying by oil and gas companies, and called into question the established understandings of whale behaviour around ice. They also challenged the assessment by the u.s. National Marine Fisheries Service on whale stock numbers, drawing attention to the fact that whales would be found under the ice and that they were perfectly capable, like a submarine, of puncturing sea ice up to 1 m (3 ft) thick.[7]

Learning from indigenous peoples, including their adaptive strategies developed over centuries, has taken on a greater urgency in an era of a warming Arctic and global environmental change. The development of respectful relationships has been the hallmark of more recent research, some of which were further publicized and supported in the 2007–8 International Polar Year. Formal consultation and the co-production of knowledge is now the norm for much of this endeavour in comparison to an earlier era of non-indigenous experimentation on indigenous peoples, including one of the most egregious episodes of Cold War Arctic experimentation. In 1956–7, the u.s. Air Force Aeromedical Laboratory used radioactive iodine (a medical tracer designed to measure thyroid activity) to investigate how human beings adapted to the cold. Involving around a hundred indigenous people from the Inupiat villages of Wainwright, Point Lay and Anaktuvik Pass, and Athabascan Indian villages of Fort Yukon and Arctic Village, military scientists were interested in the role that the thyroid gland might play in cold-weather adaptation.[8] The bodies of Arctic peoples became yet another site for Western experimentation. While Shelley's Frankenstein might have imagined it, u.s. military scientists experimented on living flesh.

What has changed from those Cold War days of military experimentation and transplantation to urban communities and associated residential schools is that indigenous peoples in the Arctic are adapting to living inside the national jurisdictions of Arctic states while demanding their rights as indigenous peoples as noted in the UN Declaration on the Rights of Indigenous Peoples. While the fate of native peoples is varied, the most progress regarding land and resource rights and political consultation and engagement has been made in Alaska, Canada and Scandinavia. In Russia, the picture is more mixed and indigenous peoples face marginalization and in some cases uncertain access to traditional herding areas in the face of growing demands for mining and military related projects in the far north. Climate change and enhanced global geopolitical interest in the Arctic are complicating factors, as indigenous peoples continue to push for recognition and respect of their historic and cultural rights to lands and resources, including hunting whales, reindeer, caribou, polar bears, seals and walruses. While native peoples of the Arctic have shown an extraordinary ability to adapt to change, it is noticeable that they are overwhelmingly minority communities, with the sole exception of Greenland.

When all else goes wrong, we might return once again to cold environments for some sort of comfort from the vagaries of human life including indigenous struggles. Buried within the permanent ice of the northern Norwegian archipelago of Svalbard lies a vault filled with samples of the world's seeds. Opened in 2008 and funded by the Norwegian government, it is known as the 'Doomsday Vault' because it contains seeds from geopolitically vulnerable countries such as Afghanistan and Iraq and other areas of the world at risk from violent events including storms and hurricanes. Tunnelled 125 m (410 ft) into a mountain, it is lined with concrete walls and equipped with blast-proof doors. It is located 130 m (426 ft) above sea level to ensure that meltwater flooding should not be a hazard.[9] What should concern us is why we feel the need to have created it in the first place. How are we humans (and non-humans) going to cope with a world where climate and societal drivers are melting large bodies of ice and snow? What will be the impact of the subsequent altering of circulatory patterns of heat, resource-led development, disrupted food chains, sea-level rise and severe winter storms on coastal communities around the Arctic?

Ice, snow and biosphere

In ice and snow environments, there are indigenous and alien species of flora and fauna. Norwegian whalers working on the sub-Antarctic island of South Georgia deliberately introduced some alien species such as reindeer while others arrived by accident, blown there by winds and/or transported there by ships through ballast water discharge. As polar waters warm, those invasive species such as the European Green Crab and Japanese Ghost Shrimp are increasingly likely to survive due to human shipping practices. Fish migration will alter as well, as new species such as mackerel are now being caught off the coastline of Greenland. We are learning through careful research, long-term observation and in consultation with indigenous peoples ever more about non-human communities that have made ice and snow an integral part of their existence. The overall picture is one where there are few areas of the cryosphere that have not been colonized by some combination of people, animals and plants. The overall warming being experienced in the Arctic, the Antarctic and mountainous regions makes it more likely that alien species invasion could occur. Rising tourist numbers are a contributory factor and one recent study estimated that perhaps as many as 70,000 seeds were being brought into Antarctica via visitor clothing, shoes and luggage including backpacks in one summer season.[10]

Snow and ice define alpine and polar environments and play a distinct and multi-faceted role in facilitating, blocking and regulating flora and fauna. Snow cover provides insulation and protection for some plants, animals and soil. Snow and ice also present challenges to animals and plants, and some have adapted specifically to break through or work around the presence of ice. Reindeer and caribou have powerful hooves that enable them to penetrate ice and expose essential food supplies of lichen and moss. This adaptive practice has allowed reindeer husbandry to develop and become integral to Sámi across northern Scandinavia and northwest Russia. The future health of this communal activity depends on the state of snow, permafrost and lake and river ice, which informs the feeding, migratory and reproduction

Svalbard Global Seed Vault.

cycles of reindeer. One noticeable strategy used by herders is to ensure that the strongest male reindeer are used strategically to break up the hardest patches of ice so that other members of the herd can access plants and pasture below. Sámi reindeer herding is traditionally a cross-border enterprise, however, and arguably the greatest short-term challenge is the policies and practices of Arctic states, which have their own resource agendas (often based on the extractive sector) and protocols that can influence the capacity of indigenous peoples to profit from reindeer meat, carving and fur sales.[11]

For plants, the longevity of ice and snow cover determines growing seasons, and snow and ice melt determine water release and soil infiltration. For many ecosystems dominated by ice and snow, the change can be dramatic when ice turns back to water. Far from being akin to a tap gently releasing water back into the environment, the melting of ice and snow can be dangerous and overwhelming. Flooding is common in many alpine and polar environments and many northern states of America can attest to the costly consequences of ice melt. Frozen and/or semi-frozen ground is not ideal when it comes to infiltration, acting in effect

like concrete and tarmac in urban environments. Water run-off causes flooding and downstream chaos. Plants and shrubs can become waterlogged and ruined.

Reindeer farm, Inari, Finland.

In the marine environment, the distribution and thickness of sea ice is pivotal to the lives of polar bears and others including seals and whales. For some animals, hibernation and migration are the preferred strategy of survival. In winter, ice and snow make it harder for most animals and humans to move about and near total darkness is prevalent in higher latitudes. In order to save energy, Caribou walk in single file so that the lead mature animal helps to clear a path for those following behind, especially the young. Birds and whales migrate to new feeding grounds, including Antarctica in the case of the ultra-long-distance flyer, the Arctic Tern. Polar and brown bears hibernate until the onset of spring and deer and elk armed with their thick winter coats of fur simply migrate to lower-lying valleys.

In areas dominated by permafrost, plants and forests can endure frozen ground because they have adapted to coping with little fresh water during the winter. Surface vegetation protects in turn the permafrost from more substantial melting. The root structures are also able, where necessary, to draw upon ground water below the frozen topsoil. In the summer season, these environments often resemble bogs, as surface water develops after spring melting. The release of water, in combination with nutrient release, encourages in many parts of the northern latitudes immense boreal and/or taiga forestry: conifer trees rooted in an environment which is swampy, moist, and filled with midges and mosquitos. Warming can also lead to fungal and insect infestation and large areas of boreal forest in Canada and Russia have been destroyed by disease. If the permafrost is disturbed, however, by fire, excess melting or human intervention then the resident plants and forestry can also be disrupted, in some cases leading to collapse of trees ('drunk forests') as more frequent freeze–thaw events disrupt the frozen layer and unsettle root structures. While drought in forests is alleviated by spring melt, heavy snowfall in winter can also destroy tree canopies and block new spring growth.

Flora and fauna that live with ice and snow will be forced to adapt and adjust to a series of drivers of change ranging from temperature and sea-level rises to expanding industrial and resource-led activity.[12] Population change is also likely and northern cities and towns are witnessing increasing numbers, most of whom will be migrants from other parts of the world. Of all the areas of the cryosphere, it is increasingly likely that the Arctic will be at the forefront of continued change and development. The Antarctic will remain largely free from human communities other than scientists and tourists in the foreseeable future. Warming will bring opportunities and dangers, new flora and fauna will make the regions like the Arctic their home, including migrating fish stocks and accidental introduction by human activity such as ballast discharge.

Over millennia animals living with ice and snow have developed three basic strategies to cope with the shift to and from frozen water and the intense cold – disappear and return, hibernate and re-emerge, and/or seasonal adjustment. Humans have largely followed suit – they disappear to warmer climes, they 'hibernate', and/or they find ways to move around ice and snow

– all with varying degrees of agency and accomplishment. So skiing might be fun for many who live outside ice-covered areas, but for those who live with ice it is essential to mobility, survival and community resilience.

Anchored in ice and snow

Any history of our cities and towns, regardless of location, will always necessitate taking into account the infrastructure and services that made dense forms of human habitation possible. They may not be glamorous but roads, sewers, power grids, rubbish collection, pavements and lighting play a crucial role in allowing humans to live, work and move safely and securely. Adjusting to seasonal fluctuations in heat and cold is strongly reflected in the formal architecture of towns and cities, as well as management practices designed to address the vagaries of weather including ice and snow. Winter storms dump huge quantities of snow on cities such as New York, disrupting essential services such as water provision, transport and postal services. In 1741 a storm froze rivers and disrupted port activity in New York and Boston with knock-on effects for trade, restocking and travel. City residents began to engage in what we would now called cold-weather preparation, stockpiling wood and food for the winter months and changing where possible wheels for skis on coaches and carts. Winter weather forecasting became more systematic and communicable in the mid-nineteenth century through news media such as telegraph broadcasts and newspapers.

European and North American cities began experimenting with snow flattening and later ploughing in pioneering Milwaukee in 1862.[13] In the case of the Minnesotan city, horses pulled along a makeshift snowplough – this represented the first formal act of recognition by a city authority that snow removal and ice clearance was a civic responsibility. Previously, snow and ice clearance was more informal, with the onus on citizens to take responsibility for their street. The instigation of a snowplough service was part of a suite of actions taken by larger cities to respond to winter weather. Revised building standards were better adjusted to the dangers posed by accumulated snow and the potential impact of ice storms on exposed city infrastructure and communication networks such as telegraph poles. Winter storm damage also carried with it the risk of fire so city planners were forced to think of how to ensure that some form of fire service could operate in cold, dark and icy conditions. Snow-ploughing was critical in ensuring some form of access to the major areas of the city but at the same time also obscured and obstructed other parts of the city as snow and ice was dumped in side streets and public spaces.

By the late nineteenth century, New York, Chicago and other major cities had established elevated transport networks to ensure that they were not choked by ice and snow, and employed snow removers to ensure that excess snow was dumped into the rivers. The so-called Great Blizzard of March 1888 hit the Eastern Seaboard with such ferocity that it led to 20-m (65-ft) drifts of snow after three days of snow and freezing ice. Cities such as New York and Boston were paralysed by the icy on-slaught, with infrastructure overwhelmed. Schools shut, fire stations were abandoned and power lines ravaged. Elevated rail-way systems were also affected. The storms claimed the lives of over four hundred but led to further recognition that wintering cities would need to do more in terms of snow and ice resilience. Electrical and communication utilities were buried below ground and underground railways and subways were constructed and opened in New York in 1894 and Boston in 1899. While commuters might have complained of stifling heat in the summer, the subways were designed to protect from excess cold, snow, wind and ice. Snow removal was further regulated, regularized and professionalized as New York City officials recognized that low-lying Brooklyn was extremely vulnerable to flooding from snow and ice melt.

Twentieth-century innovations were made in snow and ice management as city planners and their scientific advisors better appreciated the consequences and knock-on effects of excessive snow and ice. For example, snow surveys were conducted on the advice of the Michigan-born James Church (1869–1959), who

THE BLIZZARD OF MARCH 11TH, 12TH, AND 13TH, 1888.
PHOTOGRAPHS TAKEN JUST AFTER THE STORM, BY LANGILL.

pioneered the so-called Mount Rose snow sampler designed to assess snow-water content.[14] Working around Lake Tahoe in Nevada, he linked the state of snow courses to shifts in water levels and thus developed a predictive tool that was adopted by federal authorities. Church's work on snow hydrology and snowmelt management was critical in the prediction of snow melting and its implications for wastewater management. And the city of Detroit was the first to pioneer rock salt, spreading it on roads in 1940, a decision made easier by the proximity of a large salt mine served by the Detroit Salt Company. Salt works by lowering the freezing temperature of water, and thus slowing down freezing. In 2015 alone, 15 million tonnes of rock salt were applied to America's roads, while billions of dollars are spent in the aftermath, cleaning up the debris of salt including

Great Winter Blizzard of March 1888 that hit North American cities such as New York.

water pollution and salt corrosion damage to infrastructure and vehicles. It is now recognized that rock salt application is not quite the miracle intervention it once appeared.[15]

If rock salt was aiding and abetting America's highway system in the post-1945 era, the application of the de-icing substance glycol (mixed with hot water) on aircraft revolutionized winter travel. Federal Aviation Authority regulations were tightened to ensure that planes did not take off with frost, ice and snow attached to them because of the danger posed to safety. Airport authorities, like cities and towns, already used snowploughs to clear runways and erected snow fences to attempt to block the path of snowdrifts. While severe weather can, even to this day, delay and prevent planes from flying, the application of glycol in the 1950s finally replaced the need to clear excess ice and snow by hand, which was a time-consuming and inefficient practice clearly not suited to the advent of mass air transportation. The Munich air disaster of February 1958, where 23 people died, was initially thought to have been caused by ice forming on the wings of the aircraft.[16] Later, another menace was identified, namely slush, which prevented the aircraft from gaining sufficient take-off speed. But the dangers of ice for flying aircraft have not been totally removed, as subsequent disasters demonstrated, including Air Ontario Flight 1363 that crashed in March 1989, killing 24 people; excess ice on the wings was subsequently held responsible for the plane's failure to take off safely. Other ice-related disasters have followed in the wake of Flight 1363, most of which have involved a combination of human error, poor ice and snow clearance, and severe weather.

Our cities and critical infrastructure such as airports and power supplies have had to innovate and adapt as the demands and expectations we have for uninterrupted circulation continue unabated. Cities have been designed with covered walkways, satellites provide real-time weather predictions, and local and national authorities regulate and administer a bewildering array of cold-weather practices ranging from building standards, emergency services, public liability, water-supply management and citizen safety.[17] Cities now routinely have cold-weather plans; national governments fund and support winter weather advisory services; and local authorities advise citizens about severe winter weather and provide glossaries explaining what terms like 'wind chill' mean and the differences between freezing rain, sleet, ice storms and heavy snow.

Notwithstanding cold-weather planning and the regularization of ice and snow management, we are still heavily dependent on elemental resources such as rock salt and, more recently, foodstuffs such as beet juice and cheese rind for road-ice management. Snowploughing for most city and national authorities remains an extensive and costly business, where we are increasingly recognizing the 'hidden costs' of salt pollution and corrosive damage. It all seems a far cry from the vision of the German-born architect and engineer Otto Frei, who envisaged in 1970 an audacious plan for covered cities under inflatable high domes extending up to 800 m (2,600 ft) and designed to encapsulate up to 40,000 people living in a snow-protected environment.[18] While his vision for a dome city found a smaller-scale outlet in the form of the athletic facilities' roof structure for the 1972 Summer Olympics and the South Pole Station in Antarctica, his vision of a populace protected from the elemental dangers of ice and snow remains the ultimate in high modernist frontier architecture, betraying a relentless optimism that extreme-environment living was within reach. It didn't work out, but as the American architect Richard Buckminster Fuller once noted, people might move into domes when it becomes imperative do so.[19] But whether that would be a life worth living even if we could cytogenetically preserve ourselves is another matter.

Farewell to Ice

As our planet continues to warm and the ice continues to melt, a domed rather than doomed city harnessing solar energy and artificial water production might not seem that unappealing. While it is premature to issue a 'farewell to ice', *natural* ice is an utterly beguiling substance. It can appear as hard as concrete but then soft and fragile in a proverbial blink of an eye. Natural ice's extent and permanence will in this century be something that is talked about a great deal more. The tone of the conversation is likely to be less focused on wonder and enjoyment and rather more tilted towards risk, hazard and a profound sense of loss.[1] We can continue to make ice and snow but for many that will not invite the same sense of awe, wonder or even fear as when we encounter it on mountains, lakes, rivers, skis and seas.

REFERENCES

Prologue

1 *The Times* (2 February 1814), p. 3.
2 Nan Shepherd, *The Living Mountain* (London, 2011), p. 4.
3 Chris Stephens, *Barbara Hepworth: Centenary* (London, 2003), p. 65.
4 Johannes Kepler, *Six Cornered Snowflake* [1611] (London, 2010).
5 Reproduced in *The Poetical Works of Henry Wadsworth Longfellow* (Boston, MA, and New York, 1890).
6 James Taylor Carson, *Making an Atlantic World: Circles, Paths, and Stories from the Colonial South* (Knoxville, TN, 2007), p. 18.
7 Judith Siefring, ed., *The Oxford Dictionary of Idioms* (Oxford, 2005).
8 Johanna Laybourn-Parry, Martyn Tranter and Andrew J. Hodson, eds, *The Ecology of Snow and Ice Environments* (Oxford, 2012), p. 10.
9 Richard Greenberg, *Unmasking Europa: The Search for Life on Jupiter's Ocean Moon* (New York, 2010), p. 233.
10 James Joyce, *The Dead* [1914] (London, 2010), p. 57.
11 Primo Levi, 'Last Christmas of the War', *New York Review of Books* (30 January 1986), www.nybooks.com.
12 Hans Christian Andersen, *The Snow Queen* (Copenhagen, 1844, originally published in Danish).
13 Joshua Blu Buhs, *Bigfoot: The Life and Times of a Legend* (Chicago, IL, 2009), p. 29.

1 A World of Ice

1 Willy Weeks, *Sea Ice* (Fairbanks, AK, 2010), p. 93.
2 Anthony Doer, *About Grace* (London, 2016), p. 157.
3 Ukichiro Nakaya, *Snow Crystals: Natural and Artificial* [1954] (Cambridge, 2013).
4 Shawn Marshall, *The Cryosphere* (Princeton, NJ, 2012), pp. 1–10.
5 California Department of Water Resources, *Sierra Nevada Snowpack is Virtually Gone; Water Content Now Is Only 5 Percent*

of Historic Average, Lowest Since 1950 (Sacramento, 1 April 2015), www.water.ca.gov.

6 Ute Christina Herzfeld, *Atlas of Antarctica* (Berlin, 2004), p. 287.

7 UNEP, *Global Outlook for Ice and Snow* (New York, 2007).

8 Marshall, *The Cryosphere*, p. 268.

9 Gino Casassa, Francisco Sepúlveda and Rolf Sinclair, eds, *The Patagonian Icefields: A Unique Natural Laboratory for Environmental and Climate Change Studies* (New York, 2012).

10 Anja Rösel, *Detection of Melt Ponds on Arctic Sea Ice with Optical Satellite Data* (Berlin, 2013), p. 15.

11 Ralph Waldo Emerson, 'The Snow-storm' (1834), reproduced in *Selected Writings of Ralph Waldo Emerson*, ed. William Gilman (New York, 2011).

12 Peter Knight, *Glaciers* (Cheltenham, 1999), p. 213.

13 Christoph Irmscher, *Louis Agassiz: Creator of American Science* (Boston, MA, 2013), pp. 41–84.

14 John Giaever, *The White Desert: The Official Account of the Norwegian-British-Swedish Antarctic Expedition* (London, 1954).

15 Richard B. Alley, *The Two-mile Time Machine: Ice Cores, Abrupt Climate Change, and Our Future* (Princeton, NJ, 2014).

16 Brian Fagan, *The Little Ice Age: How Climate Made History, 1300–1850* (London, 2002).

17 Mariana Gosnell, *Ice: The Nature, the History, and the Uses of an Astonishing Substance* (New York, 2005).

18 Mike Walker, *Quaternary Dating Methods* (Chichester, 2005), p. 241.

19 Konrad Spindler, *The Man in the Ice* (London, 2013).

2 Exploring and Conquering Ice

1 Stewart Weaver, *Exploration: A Very Short Introduction* (Oxford, 2015).

2 James Chapman, *Past and Present: National Identity and the British Historical Film* (London, 2005), pp. 143–65.

3 James Fargo Balliett, *Mountains: Environmental Issues, Global Perspectives* (London, 2010).

4 Barry Cunliffe, *The Extraordinary Voyage of Pytheas the Greek: The Man Who Discovered Britain* (London, 2002).

5 Duane W. Roller, *Through the Pillars of Herakles: Greco-Roman Exploration of the Atlantic* (London, 2006), p. 85.

6 Ibid.

7 Joanna Kavenna, *The Ice Museum: In Search of the Lost Land of Thule* (London, 2006).

8 Pliny quoted in Vincent Cassidy, *The Sea Around Them: The Atlantic Ocean, AD 1250* (Baton Rouge, LA, 1968), p. 33.

9 Marjorie O'Rourke Boyle, *Petrarch's Genius: Pentimento and Prophecy* (Berkeley, CA, 1991), p. 41.

10 Trevor Levere, *Science and the Canadian Arctic: A Century of Exploration, 1818–1918* (Cambridge, 2003), p. 4; Jen Hill, *White Horizon: The Arctic in the Nineteenth-century British Imagination* (Albany, NY, 2008).

11 Roland Huntford, *Nansen: The Explorer as Hero* (New York, 2012); Lynne Cox, *South with the Sun: Roald Amundsen, his Polar Explorations, and the Quest for Discovery* (New York, 2011).

12 Bruce Henderson, *True North: Peary, Cook, and the Race to the Pole* (New York, 2006), p. 29.

13 Wally Herbert, *Across the Top of the World* (London, 1969).

14 Beau Riffenburgh, *Shackleton's Forgotten Expedition: The Voyage of the Nimrod* (London, 2008); Max Jones, *The Last Great Quest: Captain Scott's Antarctic Sacrifice* (Oxford, 2004).

15 Robert Scott, *Scott's Last Expedition: Diaries, 26 November 1910–29 March 1912* (Stroud, 2010).

16 Douglas Mawson, *The Home of the Blizzard: Being the Story of the Australasian Antarctic Expedition, 1911–1914* (London, 1915), p. 259.

17 Maurice Herzog, *Annapurna: The First Conquest of an 8,000-metre Peak* (London, 1954).

18 Katie Ives, 'Sharp End: Off the Map', *The Alpinist* (6 November 2015).

19 Sherry Ortner, *Life and Death on Mount Everest: Sherpas and Himalayan Mountaineering* (Princeton, NJ, 2002), p. 217.

20 Daniela Liggett et al., eds, *Exploring the Last Continent: An Introduction to Antarctica* (New York, 2015).

3 Imagining and Representing Ice

1 Dan O'Neill, *The Last Giant of Beringia: The Mystery of the Bering Land Bridge* (Boulder, CO, 2004).

2 Eric Wilson, *The Spiritual History of Ice: Romanticism, Science and the Imagination* (London, 2003).

3 Han Lörzing, *The Nature of Landscape: A Personal Quest* (Rotterdam, 2001), p. 93.

4 Mary Warnock, *Imagination* (Berkeley, CA, 1978), p. 58.

5 Donald Sharpes, *Sacred Bull, Holy Cow: A Cultural Study of Civilization's Most Important Animal* (New York, 2006), p. 111.

6 Kenneth G. Pryke and Walter C. Soderlund, eds, *Profiles of Canada* (Toronto, 2003), p. 323.

7 Jonathan Oldfield and Denis Shaw, *The Development of Russian Environmental Thought* (London, 2016).

8 Burton Raffel, *Russian Poetry Under the Tsars: An Anthology* (Albany, NY, 1971), p. 58.

9 Robert Bird, *The Russian Prospero: The Creative Universe of Viacheslav Ivanov* (Madison, WI, 2006), p. 25.

10 Robert G. Weiner, ed., *Captain America and the Struggle of the Superhero: Critical Essays* (London, 2009), p. 41.

11 Anne Gjelsvik and Rikke Schubart, eds, *Women of Ice and Fire: Gender, Game of Thrones and Multiple Media Engagements* (London, 2016).

12 Frederick Burwick, ed., *The Oxford Handbook of Samuel Taylor Coleridge* (Oxford, 2012), p. 90.

13 Wilson, *The Spiritual History of Ice*, pp. 168–92.

14 Mary Wollstonecraft Shelley, *Frankenstein* (Cambridge, 1869), p. 162.

15 Adriana Craciun, *Writing Arctic Disaster: Authorship and Exploration* (Cambridge, 2016).

16 Joseph Conrad, *Complete Short Stories of Joseph Conrad (Including his Memoirs, Letters, and Critical Essays)* (ebook, 2015).

17 Jeffrey Meyers, *Joseph Conrad: A Biography* (New York, 2001), p. 213.

18 Mark Nuttall, ed., *Encyclopedia of the Arctic* (London, 2005), p. 1345.

19 Bjarne Grønnow, 'Blessings and Horrors of the Interior: Ethno-historical Studies of Inuit Perceptions Concerning the Inland Region of West Greenland', *Arctic Anthropology*, 46 (2009), pp. 191–201.

20 Julie Cruikshank, *Do Glaciers Listen? Local Knowledge, Colonial Encounters, and Social Imagination* (Vancouver, 2005).

21 Douglas Palmer, ed., *Earth Time: Exploring the Deep Past from Victorian England to the Grand Canyon* (Chichester, 2005).

22 Edmund Burke, *A Philosophical Enquiry into the Origin of Our Ideas of the Sublime and Beautiful* (London, 1757), and cited in Angela Woods, *The Sublime Object of Psychiatry: Schizophrenia in Clinical and Cultural Theory* (Oxford, 2011), p. 26.

23 Esther Leslie, *Liquid Crystals: The Science and Art of a Fluid Form* (London 2016).

24 Richard Bangs, *Quest for the Sublime: Finding Nature's Secret in Switzerland* (Birmingham, AL, 2008).

25 Peter Fjagesund, *The Dream of the North: A Cultural History to 1920* (New York, 2014), p. 329.

26 Tim Bergfelder and Sarah Street, eds, *The Titanic in Myth and Memory: Representations in Visual and Literary Culture* (London, 2004).

27 Gillian Steinberg, *Thomas Hardy: The Poems* (Basingstoke, 2013), p. 97.

28 Joe Simpson, *Touching the Void* (London, 1988).

29 James Balog and Terry Williams, *Ice: Portraits of Vanishing Glaciers* (New York, 2012).
30 Bruce Robbins, 'The Sweatshop Sublime', PMLA, 117 (2002), pp. 84–97.

4 **Icy Geopolitics**

1 Halford Mackinder, 'The Geographical Pivot of History', *Geographical Journal*, XXIII (1904), pp. 421–37.
2 Vilhjalmur Stefansson, 'The Arctic as an Air Route of the Future', *National Geographic*, 42 (August 1922), p. 205; Stefansson, *The Friendly Arctic* (New York, 1921).
3 Sverker Sörlin, ed., *Science, Geopolitics and Culture in the Polar Region: Norden Beyond Borders* (Farnham, 2013).
4 Klaus Dodds, *Pink Ice: Britain and the South Atlantic Empire* (London, 2002).
5 Dian Olson Belanger, *Deep Freeze: The United States, the International Geophysical Year and the Origins of Antarctic Science* (Boulder, CO, 2006).
6 Margot Hill, *Climate Change and Water Governance: Adaptive Capacity in Chile and Switzerland* (New York, 2013), p. 126.
7 Kees Bastmeijer, ed., *Wilderness Protection in Europe: The Role of International, European and National Law* (Cambridge, 2016).
8 Laurence Boisson de Chazournes, *Fresh Water in International Law* (Oxford, 2013), p. 45.
9 Fred M. Shelley, *Nation Shapes: The Story behind the World's Borders* (Santa Barbara, CA, 2013), pp. 152 and 177.
10 United Nations Law of the Sea Convention 1982 Article 234, available at: www.un.org/depts/los/convention_agreements/texts/unclos/unclos_e.pdf.
11 Michael Byers, *International Law and the Arctic* (Cambridge, 2013), pp. 134–7.
12 Philip E. Steinberg, Jeremy Tasch and Hannes Gerhardt, *Contesting the Arctic: Rethinking Politics in the Circumpolar North* (London, 2015), p. 51.
13 See 'Our Peoples Can Live Together in Peace and Friendship', www.theguardian.com, 19 January 2004.
14 See www.paninuittrails.org, accessed 5 September 2017.
15 See http://sikuatlas.ca/index.html, accessed 5 September 2017.
16 A Circumpolar Inuit Declaration on Sovereignty in the Arctic, available at www.inuitcircumpolar.com/sovereignty-in-the-arctic.html.

5 Working with Ice

1 Dewey Hill and Elliot Hughes, *Ice Harvesting in Early America* (New Hartford, NY, 1977); Jonathan Rees, *Refrigeration Nation: A History of Ice, Appliances, and Enterprise in America* (Baltimore, MD, 2013).

2 Carroll Gantz, *Refrigeration: A History* (Jefferson, NC, 2015), p. 28.

3 Gavin Weightman, *The Frozen Water Trade* (London, 2010).

4 Felicity Kinross, *Coffee and Ices: The Story of Carlo Gatti in London* (Sudbury, 1991).

5 Mark Kurlansky, *Frozen in Time: Clarence Birdseye's Outrageous Idea About Frozen Food* (New York, 2014).

6 Andrew F. Smith, *Eating History: 30 Turning Points in the Making of American Cuisine* (New York, 2009), pp. 165–74.

7 Diane Boucher, *The 1950s American Home* (London, 2013).

8 David Christopher, *British Culture* (London, 1999), p. 118.

9 Iceland Frozen Foods Company, 'The Iceland Story', available at http://about.iceland.co.uk/about-iceland/the-iceland-story.

10 Terry McFadden and Lawrence Bennett, *Construction in Cold Regions: A Guide for Planners, Engineers, Contractors and Managers* (Chichester, 1991).

11 National Research Council (U.S.), Panel on Snow Avalanches, *Snow Avalanche Hazards and Mitigation in the United States* (Washington, DC, 1990).

12 Ainsley Doty, 'Buried Alive: An Avalanche Survivor Breaks his Silence', *Maclean's* (29 March 2015), www.macleans.ca.

13 Shiva Pudasaini and Kolumban Hutter, *Avalanche Dynamics: Dynamics of Rapid Flows of Dense Granular Avalanches* (New York, 2007), p. 514.

14 The main professional body in the United States is the American Society of Civil Engineers, Cold Regions Engineering Division, www.asce.org/cold-regions-engineering/cold-regions-engineering.

15 U.S. Forest Service National Avalanche Center, www.fsavalanche.org.

16 Graydon Allen Tunstall, *Blood on the Snow: The Carpathian Winter War of 1915* (Lawrence, 2010); Mark Thompson, *The White War: Life and Death on the Italian Front, 1915–1919* (London, 2009).

17 Wilhelm Dege, *War North of 80: The Last German Arctic Weather Station of World War II* (Calgary, 2009).

18 Laurel J. Hummel, *Alaska's Militarized Landscape: The Unwritten Legacy of the Cold War* (Boulder, CO, 2002).

19 David Day, *Antarctica* (Oxford, 2013), p. 382.

20 Matti Leppäranta, *The Drift of Sea Ice* (New York, 2011), p. 3.

21 Ibid., p. 12.

22 Nikolai Zubov, *Arctic Ice* (Washington, DC, 1963).

23 William Leary, *Under Ice: Waldo Lyon and the Development of the Arctic Submarine* (College Station, TX, 1999).

24 National Academy of Sciences National Research Council, *Arctic Sea Ice: Proceedings of the Conference* (Washington, DC, 1958).

25 Elana Wilson Rowe, ed., *Russia and the North* (Ottawa, 2009).

26 Ingvild Ulrikke Jakobsen, *Marine Protected Areas in International Law: An Arctic Perspective* (Leiden, 2016), p. 316.

6 Sport, Leisure and Pleasure on Ice

1 Simon Hudson, *Snow Business: A Study of the International Ski Industry* (London, 2000).

2 Gib Goodfellow, *Building an Ice Hotel* (London, 2004).

3 Roland Huntford, *Two Planks and a Passion: The Dramatic History of Skiing* (London, 2009).

4 John Fry, *The Story of Modern Skiing* (Dartmouth, NH, 2006), p. 12.

5 Vivien Bowers, *In the Path of an Avalanche: A True Story* (Vancouver, 2003), p. 74.

6 Fry, *The Story of Modern Skiing*, p. 8.

7 OECD, *Climate Change in the European Alps Adapting Winter Tourism and Natural Hazards Management* (Paris, 2007), p. 45.

8 Annie Gilbert Coleman, *Ski Style: Sport and Culture in the Rockies* (Lawrence, KS, 2004), p. 35.

9 Elizabeth Burakowski and Matthew Magnusson, *Climate Impacts on the Winter Tourism Economy in the United States* (Hanover, 2012), www.nrdc.org.

7 Adapting to Ice

1 Erik R. Swenson and Peter Bärtsch, eds, *High Altitude: Human Adaptation to Hypoxia* (New York, 2013), p. 211.

2 Arctic Council, *Snow, Water, Ice, Permafrost in the Arctic Report* (Tromsø, 2011).

3 Mariana Gosnell, *Ice: The Nature, the History, and the Uses of an Astonishing Substance* (New York, 2005).

4 Truth and Reconciliation Commission of Canada, *Canada's Residential Schools: The Inuit and Northern Experience* (Ottawa, 2016).

5 Gary Ferraro, *Cultural Anthropology: An Applied Perspective* (Belmont, CA, 2008), p. 328.

6 Igor Krupnik et al., eds, SIKU: *Knowing Our Ice: Documenting Inuit Sea Ice Knowledge and Use* (New York, 2010).

7 Mark Nuttall, *Protecting the Arctic: Indigenous Peoples and Cultural Survival* (London, 1998), p. 135.

8 Barbara Rose Johnston, *Half-lives and Half-truths: Confronting the Radioactive Legacies of the Cold War* (Santa Fe, NM, 2007), p. 38.

9 Cary Fowler, *Seeds on Ice: Svalbard and the Global Seed Vault* (New Haven, CT, 2016).

10 David W. H. Walton, ed., *Antarctica: Global Science from a Frozen Continent* (Cambridge, 2013).

11 Christina Allard and Susann Funderud Skogvang, eds, *Indigenous Rights in Scandinavia: Autonomous Sami Law* (Farnham, 2015).

12 Arnoldus Schytte Blix, *Arctic Animals and their Adaptations to Life on the Edge* (Trondheim, 2005).

13 Blake McKelvey, *Snow in the Cities: A History of America's Urban Response* (Rochester, NY, 1995), pp. 67–9.

14 Roger Barry and Thian Yew Gan, *The Global Cryosphere: Past, Present and Future* (Cambridge, 2011), p. 11.

15 John Thornes, Len Wood and Robert Blackmore, 'To Salt or not to Salt?', *New Scientist* (10 February 1977).

16 Stephen Morrin, *The Munich Air Disaster* (London, 2007).

17 John Levy, *Contemporary Urban Planning* (New York, 2016), pp. 182–3.

18 Julie Decker, *Modern North: Architecture on the Frozen Edge* (New York, 2010), p. 13.

19 Tim McKeough, 'What can We Learn from Buckminster Fuller', 23 August 2007, www.wired.com

Farewell to Ice

1 Peter Wadhams, *A Farewell to Ice* (London, 2016).

SELECT BIBLIOGRAPHY

Agassiz, Louis, *Études sur les glaciers* (Paris, 2015)

Anderson, Alun, *After the Ice: Life, Death and Geopolitics in the New Arctic* (London, 2009)

Banerjee, Sanjay, *Arctic Voices: Resistance at the Tipping Point* (New York, 2012)

Beatie, Andrew, *The Alps: A Cultural History* (New York, 2006)

Benn, Douglas, and David Evans, *Glaciers and Glaciation* (London, 2010)

Bennett, Matthew, and Neil Glasser, eds, *Glacial Geology: Ice Sheets and Landforms* (Oxford, 2009)

Bentley, Wilson, *Snow Crystals* (New York, 1931)

Berton, Pierre, *The Arctic Grail: The Quest for the Northwest Passage and the North Pole, 1818–1909* (New York, 1988)

Cherry-Gerrard, Apsley, *The Worst Journey in the World* (London, 2010)

Cosgrove, Denis, and Veronica della Dora, eds, *High Places: Cultural Geographies of Mountains, Ice and Science* (London, 2009)

Cruikshank, Julie, *Do Glaciers Listen? Local Knowledge, Colonial Encounters, and Social Imagination* (Vancouver, 2005)

David, Robert, *The Arctic in the British Imagination, 1818–1914* (Manchester, 2000)

Davidson, Peter, *The Idea of the North* (London, 2016)

Decker, Julie, *True North: Contemporary Art of the Circumpolar North* (Anchorage, AK, 2012)

Della Dora, Veronica, *Mountains* (London, 2016)

Denning, Andrew, *Skiing into Modernity* (Berkeley, CA, 2014)

Dodds, Klaus, and Mark Nuttall, *The Scramble for the Poles* (Cambridge, 2016)

Emmerson, Charles, *The Future History of the Arctic* (London, 2011)

Fox, William, *Terra Antarctica: Looking into the Emptiest Continent* (San Antonio, TX, 2005)

Fuchs, Vivian, and Edmund Hillary, *The Crossing of Antarctica* (London, 1959)

Grace, Sherrill, *Canada and the Idea of the North* (Montreal and Kingston, 2007)

Haines, Brigid, *The Ice and the Inland: Mawson, Flynn, and the Myth of the Frontier* (Melbourne, 2002)

Hansen, Peter, *The Summits of Modern Man: Mountaineering after the Enlightenment* (Cambridge, 2013)

Holman, Andrew, eds, *Canada's Game: Hockey and Identity* (Montreal and Kingston, 2009)

Jones, Max, *The Last Great Quest: Captain Scott's Antarctic Sacrifice* (Oxford, 2004)

Krakauer, John, *Into Thin Air* (London, 2011)

Leane, Elizabeth, *South Pole* (London, 2016)

Libbrecht, Kenneth, *Ken Libbrecht's Field Guide to Snowflakes* (New York, 2006)

Lopez, Barry, *Arctic Dreams* (London, 2014)

McCannon, John, *Red Arctic: Polar Exploration and the Myth of the North in the Soviet Union, 1932–1939* (Oxford, 1997)

—, *A History of the Arctic: Nature, Exploration and Exploitation* (London, 2012)

MacFarlane, Robert, *Mountain of the Mind* (London, 2008)

Martin-Nielsen, Janet, *Eismitte in the Scientific Imagination: Knowledge and Politics at the Centre of Greenland* (London, 2013)

Pollack, Henry, *A World Without Ice* (New York, 2009)

Ponting, Herbert, *The Great White South* (New York, 2001)

Potter, Russell, *Arctic Spectacle: A Frozen North in Visual Culture, 1818–1875* (Seattle, WA, 2007)

Pyne, Stephen, *Ice: A Journey to Antarctica* (Iowa City, IA, 1986)

Roberts, David, *Alone on the Ice* (New York, 2014)

Robinson, Michael, *The Coldest Crucible: Arctic Exploration and American Culture* (Chicago, IL, 2010)

Shepherd, Nan, *The Living Mountain: A Celebration of the Cairngorm Mountains of Scotland* (London, 2011)

Smith, Michael, *Shackleton: By Endurance We Conquer* (Oxford, 2015)

Spufford, Francis, *I May Be Some Time: Ice and the English Imagination* (London, 2003)

—, and Elizabeth Kolbert, eds, *The Ends of the Earth* (New York, 2007)

Thoreau, Henry David, *Walden* (New York, 2009)

Wheeler, Sara, *Terra Incognita: Travels in Antarctica* (London, 1997)

Whiteman, Colin, *Cold Region Hazards and Risks* (Oxford, 2011)

Whitson, David, and Richard Gruneau, *Artificial Ice: Hockey, Culture, and Commerce* (Calgary, 2006)

Wilke, Sabine, *German Culture and the Modern Environmental
Imagination: Narrating and Depicting Nature* (Leiden, 2015)
Wilson, Eric, *The Spiritual History of Ice: Romanticism, Science
and Imagination* (London, 2003)
Woodward, Jamie, *The Ice Age* (Oxford, 2014)

ASSOCIATIONS AND WEBSITES

This list gives an indication of the array of institutions that address ice and snow in some form without claiming to be comprehensive.

Alfred Wegner Institute
www.awi.de/en

Alpine Club
www.alpine-club.org.uk

Alpine Journal
www.alpinejournal.org.uk

American Alpine Club
https://americanalpineclub.org

Antarctic Glaciers
www.antarcticglaciers.org

Antarctic Science
www.cambridge.org/core/journals/antarctic-science

Antarctic Treaty System
www.ats.aq/e/ats.htm

Arctic and Antarctic Research Institute (Russia)
www.aari.ru

Arctic Circle
www.arcticcircle.org

Arctic Council
www.arctic-council.org

Association of Early Career Polar Scientists
www.apecs.is

British Antarctic Survey
www.bas.ac.uk

British Cryogenic Council
http://bcryo.org.uk

British Library
www.bl.uk

Byrd Polar and Climate Research Center, Ohio State University
https://bpcrc.osu.edu

Cold Regions Division (CRD) of the Canadian Society for Civil
    Engineering (CSCE)
https://csce.ca/committees/cold-regions

Cold Regions Research and Engineering Laboratory
www.erdc.usace.army.mil/Locations/CRREL

Girls on Ice
http://girlsonice.org

Harbin International Ice and Snow Festival
www.chinahighlights.com/festivals/harbin-ice-and-snow-festival.htm

Institute for Snow and Avalanche Research
www.slf.ch/english_EN

International Glaciological Society
www.igsoc.org

Mountain Rescue Association
http://mra.org

National Ice and Snow Data Center
https://nsidc.org

National Institute of Polar Research (Japan)
www.nipr.ac.jp/english

National Maritime Museum
www.rmg.co.uk/national-maritime-museum

Natural Environment Research Council (NERC)
www.nerc.ac.uk

Northern Warfare Training Center
www.army.mil/article/170432

Norwegian Polar Institute
www.npolar.no/en

Polar Record
www.cambridge.org/core/journals/polar-record

Polar World
www.polarworld.co.uk

Royal Geographical Society
www.rgs.org

Sapporo Snow Festival
www.snowfes.com/english

Scientific Committee on Antarctic Research
www.scar.org

Scott Polar Research Institute, University of Cambridge
www.spri.cam.ac.uk

Snow and Ice Management Association
www.arcticcircle.org

Southampton Oceanography Centre (SOC), University of Southampton
www.noc.soton.ac.uk

Swiss Polar Institute
http://polar.epfl.ch

United Kingdom Antarctic Heritage Trust
www.ukaht.org

ACKNOWLEDGEMENTS

I have a large number of people to acknowledge in the writing and completion of this book. At Reaktion Books, Michael Leaman and Daniel Allen were immensely encouraging and gave critical yet supportive feedback at the drafting stages, Rebecca Ratnayake was a great help at the final image-related stages, and my thanks to text editor Amy Salter.

Fellow Earth series writers and Royal Holloway colleagues, Peter Adey and Veronica della Dora, provided wise consul. Another Royal Holloway colleague, Rachael Squire, was also a friendly and insightful critic as well as a great help in suggesting potential images for the book. Former Royal Holloway msc. Geopolitics and Security graduate, Alice Oates, provided invaluable research assistance at a critical stage. Jonathan Bamber, Elizabeth Leane and Peder Roberts also provided many critical insights on the manuscript. Over the years, I have also shared many conversations with other colleagues such as Michael Bravo, Sanjay Chaturvedi, Bethan Davies, Duncan Depledge, Felix Driver, Scott Elias, Philip Hatfield, Alan Hemmings, Innes Keighren, Berit Kristoffersen, Huw Lewis-Jones, Mark Nuttall, Alasdair Pinkerton, Richard Powell, Phil Steinberg, Rosanna White and Kathryn Yusoff. Stuart Elden encouraged me to write about 'icy geopolitics' over ten years ago, and unwittingly perhaps provided the genesis for this project. Further back in time, it was in 1994 that I had the privilege of having the late Denis Cosgrove as an academic mentor, and he encouraged me to think of ice in all its elemental qualities.

In May 2017 I had the opportunity to talk about the book at a workshop organized by Alex Colas at Birkbeck College. Stephanie Jones, Esther Leslie and Alex were generous discussants and provided further food for thought. None of the above bear any responsibility for mistakes and shortcomings, however.

Numerous institutions have supported my polar and ice-related research over the years and I am particularly grateful to the British

Library, National Maritime Museum, Royal Geographical Society, and Scott Polar Research Institute at the University of Cambridge. I have also benefited over the years from research funding and travel support from the Arts and Humanities Research Council, the British Academy, the Economic and Social Research Council, the Leverhulme Trust and the Royal Norwegian Embassy in London.

Thank you to all the organizations and individuals who have given their permission for the reproduction of images.

Finally, I want to thank my family for their forbearance and support. Being a bit obsessed with ice means that you really find it terribly easily to go to places either where ice is present or where it has left its mark. So travels to mountains, the polar regions and other ice 'hotspots' have been a feature of my personal and professional life for many years. I am very grateful to my wife Carolyn and my children Alex and Millie for their patience. I know I never miss an opportunity to point out evidence of past glaciation.

The book is dedicated to my Austrian mother and late father. Along with my brother we were all devotees of *Ski Sunday*. Watching the achievements of great Austrian skiers such as Franz Klammer, Annemarie Moser-Pröll and Harti Weirather provided much pleasure.

PHOTO ACKNOWLEDGEMENTS

The author and publishers wish to express their thanks to the below sources of illustrative material and/or permission to reproduce it:

Jesse Allen/NASA/EarthObservatory/University of Maryland's Global Land Cover Facility: p. 125; from Roald Amundsen: *The South Pole*, vol. II (London, 1912); courtesy Arctic Institute: p. 160; © Wilson Bentley: p. 10; © Edward Binnie: p. 117; © Bridgeman Art Library/Royal Holloway College, University of London: p. 101; British Library, London: p. 196; from Samuel Taylor Coleridge, *The Rime of the Ancient Mariner Illustrated* (New York, 1876): p. 93; courtesy Dallas Museum of Art: p. 92; Davric (Wikimedia commons): p. 115; FGO Stuart (Wikimedia commons): p. 103; from Robert Abram Batlett and Ralph T. Hale, *The Last Voyage of the Karluk: Flagship of Vilhjalmar Stefansson's Canadian Arctic Expedition of 1913–16* (Toronto, 1916): p. 110; from Charles Francis Hall, *Inuit village, Oopungnewing, near Frobisher Bay on Baffin Island, c. 1865* (New York, 1865): p. 97; Kathryn Hansen/NASA Earth Observatory: pp. 38–9; from Leonard Huxley, ed., *Scott's Last Expedition . . .* (New York, 1913): p. 104; Kunsthalle, Hamberg: p. 99; Library of Congress, Washington, DC: p. 59; Lieutenant Cindy McFee/U.S. National Oceanic and Atmospheric Administration: p. 35; from Fridtjof Nansen, *Farthest North*, vol. LI (London, 1897): p. 60; NASA/GSFC/courtesy Kimberly Casey: p. 41; NASA/JPL/DLR: p. 20; NASA/JPL/ESO: p. 128; National Science Foundation: p. 68; National Gallery of Denmark: p. 85; National Oceanic and Atmospheric Administration: p. 132; from *New York Tribune*: p. 146; from Abraham Ortelius, *Theatrum orbis terrarum* (Antwerp, 1570): pp. 12–13; John Penney/National Science Foundation: p. 77; Pointe-à-Callière Montreal Archeology and History Complex: p. 177; private collection: p. 86; Pushkin Museum, Moscow: p. 83; SA-Kuva/Finnish Wartime Photograph Archive: p. 156; Touriste (Wikimedia commons): p. 124; United States Coast Guard: p. 131; United States Patent Office: p. 145; from Jules Dumont d'Urville, *Voyage au pôle sud et dans l'océanie sur les corvettes l'astrolabe et la zélée exécuté par ordre*

Readers are free:

> to share – to copy, distribute and transmit the work
> to remix – to adapt the this image alone

Under the following conditions:

> attribution – You must attribute the work in the manner specified by the author or licensor (but not in any way that suggests that they endorse you or your use of the work).
>
> share alike – If you alter, transform, or build upon this work, you may distribute the resulting work only under the same or similar license to this one.

INDEX

Page numbers in *italics* refer to illustrations